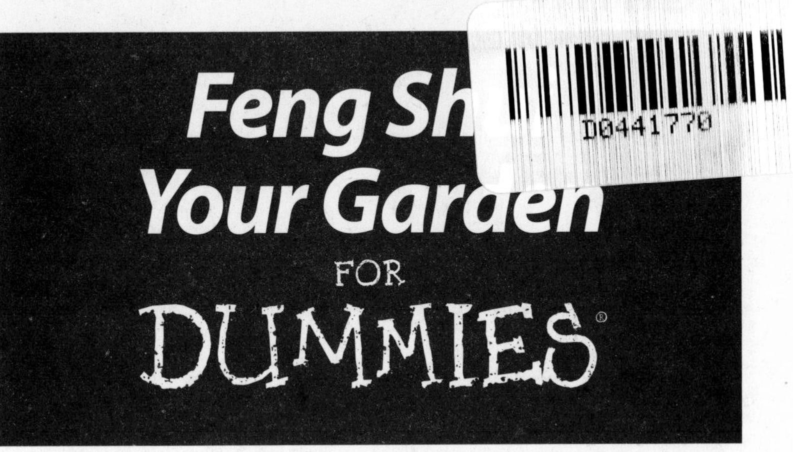

by Holly Ziegler and
Jennifer Lawler

Wiley Publishing, Inc.

Feng Shui Your Garden For Dummies®

Published by
Wiley Publishing, Inc.
111 River St.
Hoboken, NJ 07030-5774
www.wiley.com

Published by Wiley Publishing, Inc., Indianapolis, Indiana

Published simultaneously in Canada

For general information on our other products and services or to obtain technical support, please contact our Customer Care Department within the U.S. at 800-762-2974, outside the U.S. at 317-572-3993, or fax 317-572-4002.

Wiley also publishes its books in a variety of electronic formats. Some content that appears in print may not be available in electronic books.

Library of Congress Control Number: 2003115307

ISBN: 0-7645-1975-1

Manufactured in the United States of America

10 9 8 7 6 5 4 3 2 1

1B/RU/QR/QU

About the Authors

Holly Ziegler is passionate about Feng Shui and is a writer, consultant, and instructor on the subject. Since 1976, she has also been a multi-million-dollar real estate broker on California's Central Coast and recently authored *Sell Your Home Faster with Feng Shui* (Dragon Chi Pub). Somewhere in the midst of this she finds time to fulfill numerous public speaking requests and teach Feng Shui at the college level. Holly lives in the delightful town of Arroyo Grande, California, and is the proud mother of two great kids.

Jennifer Lawler is a writer and martial arts expert. She has written more than 20 books (she stopped counting birthdays and books at about the same time). She is the author of *Feng Shui Your Workspace For Dummies* and *Martial Arts For Dummies.* She lives with her adorable daughter, who raises the chi in any environment, and two rambunctious dogs (ditto).

Dedication

Holly Ziegler dedicates this book to Karin Leonard and Arlene Winn, my dear sisters of choice . . . for bringing such joy and adventure into the garden of my life. And to Jan Hayes, the secretary of my dreams, who makes my way smooth at every turn.

Jennifer Lawler dedicates this book to her parents, who taught her the joys of daffodils and dogs.

Acknowledgments

We would like to thank Tracy Boggier, our acquisitions editor, for having the vision for this book and helping us achieve it. We'd also like to thank our project editors, Jennifer Connolly and Chrissy Guthrie, and copy editor Jennifer Bingham, for all their hard work on our behalf. Without them, we would have been much, much crazier at the end of this project. Our technical reviewer, Francine Van De Vanter, also deserves our gratitude for helping us keep our facts straight.

We also want to mention that literary agent extraordinaire, Carol Susan Roth, makes all things possible.

We'd like to offer special recognition to our contributors, who helped make this book a thorough, useful tool for readers:

Jayme Barrett, best-selling author of *Feng Shui Your Life,* is a certified Feng Shui consultant specializing in energy techniques for personal fulfillment, prosperity, and integrated health. She is the Mind/Body editor for *Ms. Fitness Magazine* and has appeared nationally on NBC, Style, and HGTV. Jayme consults on residential and commercial properties and lives in Los Angeles. Visit her at `www.jaymebarrett.com`.

P.K. Odle, owner of Feng Shui Advantage and worldwide instructor for Master Larry Sang's American Feng Shui Institute, has been a full-time Feng Shui practitioner since 1988. She practices classical Feng Shui. Visit her at `www.fengshuiadvantage.com`.

Herb Schaal is a landscape architect with more than 25 years of experience. Thirty of his projects have been recognized for awards by the American Society of Landscape Architects. He has been a consulting landscape architect to the Denver Botanic Garden for 20 years and is highly regarded throughout the industry for his children's gardens. He is vice president and principal of EDAW.

We must thank the Friesen family for permission to include photos of Betty Friesen's garden in this book. Other avid gardeners who let us take a look include Dena Friesen, Bridget Mahan, and Tom and Yvonne Lawler.

EDAW also graciously permitted us to reproduce some of their photographs here. EDAW can be reached at `www.edaw.com`. Those photographs are © 2004 EDAW — photography by Dixi Carrillo.

Beckett Corporation allowed us to showcase some of their water feature products, available at most major home improvement stores and many fine independent lawn and garden shops. Toll-free: 1-888-BECKETT or `www.888beckett.com`. Those photographs are © 2004 Beckett Corporation. All Rights Reserved.

Publisher's Acknowledgments

We're proud of this book; please send us your comments through our Dummies online registration form located at www.dummies.com/register/.

Some of the people who helped bring this book to market include the following:

Acquisitions, Editorial, and Media Development

Project Editors: Jennifer Connolly, Christina Guthrie

Acquisitions Editor: Tracy Boggier

Copy Editor: Jennifer Bingham

Assistant Editor: Holly Gastineau Grimes

Technical Editor: Francine Van De Vanter, ASID

Senior Permissions Editor: Carmen Krikorian

Editorial Manager: Christine Meloy Beck

Editorial Assistants: Elizabeth Rea, Melissa Bennett

Cover Photos: © Patrick Johns/CORBIS

Cartoons: Rich Tennant, www.the5thwave.com

Production

Project Coordinator: Adrienne Martinez

Layout and Graphics: Joyce Haughey, LeAndra Hosier, Michael Kruzil, Barry Offringa, Jacque Schneider

Special Art: Photographs provided by Dixi Carrillo, Beckett Corporation, and Jennifer Lawler

Proofreaders: TECHBOOKS Production Services

Indexer: TECHBOOKS Production Services

Special Help: Michelle Dzurny

Publishing and Editorial for Consumer Dummies

Diane Graves Steele, Vice President and Publisher, Consumer Dummies

Joyce Pepple, Acquisitions Director, Consumer Dummies

Kristin A. Cocks, Product Development Director, Consumer Dummies

Michael Spring, Vice President and Publisher, Travel

Brice Gosnell, Associate Publisher, Travel

Kelly Regan, Editorial Director, Travel

Publishing for Technology Dummies

Andy Cummings, Vice President and Publisher, Dummies Technology/General User

Composition Services

Gerry Fahey, Executive Director of Production Services

Debbie Stailey, Director of Composition Services

Contents at a Glance

Table of Contents

Introduction

You stroll out into your backyard. You see a tangle of overgrown shrubs, a lawn that needed to be mowed yesterday, and a series of rosebushes minus the roses. You know that something has to be done, and soon, but you're not quite sure what or how.

Or maybe you've just taken possession of your brand-new house in a brand-new subdivision, and when you step out the back door, all you see before you is a vista of . . . sod. And in the far distance, the neighbor's sapling. Again, you're just not sure where to start.

Feng Shui (pronounced *fung-schway*) has the answer. Feng Shui is an ancient Chinese philosophy of design that can be applied to any room, building, or outdoor space. (In fact, it started out as a way to choose the most auspicious outdoor location for placing important public buildings.)

Feng Shui doesn't require burning incense or belief in bizarre, esoteric ideas. It's just a way of looking at the world and shaping your environment to be pleasing and welcoming to you. You don't even have to believe in it for it to work.

About This Book

You've got a garden, or a backyard (or a front yard or both), or at least a slab of outdoor space somewhere, or you wouldn't have picked this book up in the first place. And you need some help (we're just guessing).

Maybe you know a little about Feng Shui as it applies to your home or office, and you're curious about how it may apply to outdoor spaces — such as you garden (or at least that little plot of land that you envision as a garden). You asked, we answered.

This book offers practical advice for creating the garden of your dreams, and it gives you step-by-step instructions for overcoming challenges that may confront you. The book covers the basic principles of Feng Shui and applies them to gardening.

Conventions Used in This Book

When writing this book, we used the following conventions, and we want to make sure that you're aware of them before you start reading:

- We sometimes use foreign words or terms you may not have come across before. When we do that, we put the term in *italics* the first chance we get, and then we give you a definition.
- Whenever we talk about a subject we've covered more completely somewhere else in the book, we provide a cross reference to that chapter. We do this so we don't have to keep repeating ourselves. (And so you won't have to keep listening to the same old, same old.)
- Whenever we have a photograph or illustration we'd like you to take a glance at, we direct you to it by saying something along the lines of, "See Figure 2-1." That means to look at the first illustration in the second chapter, which is neatly labeled, "Figure 2-1." We do the same for tables (except we say, "Table 2-1").
- Any e-mail addresses or Web sites that we mention appear in `monofont` to help them stand out.

What You're Not to Read

Well, we'd love for you to read every single word of this fine book. After all, we worked really hard on it. However, if you're in a hurry, or just don't have much of an attention span, you can skip certain parts.

Anytime a paragraph has the Technical Stuff icon attached, you can skip it and still understand what's going on. You can also skip the sidebars (they appear in a gray box) because they discuss nonessential info that's related to the topic at hand. Again, we'd love for you to read them, but you don't have to. They can deepen your understanding of the topic, but they're not essential.

Foolish Assumptions

We made some assumptions about you when we were writing this book. Here are a few of them:

- You have a yard, garden, or piece of outdoor space somewhere.
- You know your surroundings influence how you feel.
- You're interested in designing a friendly, welcoming outdoor space.
- You want to do well in your life.

How This Book Is Organized

We actually put some thought into how this book was put together. We tried to organize it in such a way that the information is easy to find and easy to use. (Except for the part where you have to dig large holes in your back yard to plant trees. We're pretty sure that's hard.) We divided the book into five parts. Each part has chapters that are related to that general topic (chapters are listed in the Table of Contents).

Part I: Planting the Seeds of Feng Shui: Principles of Feng Shui

In Part I, we start at the beginning and go over the basic principles of Feng Shui. We define some key terms such as chi, Bagua, yin/yang, and the Five Elements.

We give you a bit of background on the various schools of Feng Shui and tell you about Black Hat Sect, which is the school this book follows, as do its companion texts *Feng Shui For Dummies,* by David Daniel Kennedy, and *Feng Shui Your Workspace For Dummies,* by us. (Both are published by Wiley Publishing, Inc.)

We give you some hints about getting the energy flowing in your garden (can you feel those good vibes?) and describe how all the principles of Feng Shui work together, so you can create a garden of your dreams.

Part II: Getting Started on Your Feng Shui Garden

In Part II, we show you how to plan your Feng Shui garden from step one. We give you some ideas about how to decide on the function of your garden. (Are you planning to use it for quiet contemplation or tossing around footballs? Or both?) We also guide you in choosing *auspicious* (favorable) locations for your garden and give you some ideas about what to do if you're stuck with a not-so-great location.

This part also reveals how to apply the life sectors of the Bagua to your garden so that you can increase abundance and prosperity, not just in your garden, but also in your life. We also clue you in on how to garden the natural way, which is very Feng Shui.

Then, we give you some strategies for making a garden that looks appealing in all seasons. (Okay, okay, in the dead of winter it may not look so great, but we do our best to show you how to make your garden look good even then.)

Finally, we point out how to plan and maintain a garden according to your skill level and how to tailor a garden to fit the time and money you have.

Part III: Harvesting the Blessings of Feng Shui

Here's where we give you the scoop on how to handle specific Feng Shui challenges in the garden. We give you our very best advice on choosing the best plants for your garden. Because we want you to have abundance and prosperity (not to mention a great garden and happy visitors in it), we show you how to avoid creating negative energy with your plants. We also show you how to raise the living energy by inviting wildlife into your garden.

Then we show you how to cure common Feng Shui problems, such as depressed energy, with easy-to-use cures that don't take too much time, energy, or money. We also tell you how to use intentions to bring blessings and abundance into your Feng Shui garden and your life!

Part IV: Thematically Speaking: Feng Shui and Theme Gardens

In this part, we show you how to create a theme garden that still maintains good energy flow and follows the principles of Feng Shui. We give you plenty of options to choose from and how-to-get-started information for

- Aromatherapy-herbal gardens
- Hummingbird gardens
- Butterfly gardens
- Zen gardens
- Taoist gardens
- Kitchen gardens

And we conclude the part with information on gardening in tight spaces such as patios, rooftops, courtyards, and the like.

Part V: The Part of Tens

In this part, we give you three top ten lists for quick reference. We show you how to increase abundance, fix chi flow problems, and create harmony (in your garden, anyway).

Our pointers are simple and straightforward, so you can put them to use right away.

Icons Used in This Book

In the margins of the book, we use a few different icons to identify material that you can use to better understand the principles of Feng Shui:

This icon warns you that a certain strategy, placement, or approach is *not* good Feng Shui and should be avoided as *inauspicious* (unfavorable — in other words, bad news). This icon also alerts you to potential health or safety hazards, such as inviting bees into the garden when you're allergic to bees.

This icon is used to indicate important Feng Shui principles and strategies, especially how to apply them to your particular situation. If you can only remember a few things you read in this book, remember these.

This icon is used to highlight suggestions that make your garden the most gorgeous, welcoming, abundant place possible. Most tips come from real Feng Shui practice.

This icon points out information that's interesting but nonessential to the topic at hand. Read these paragraphs, and you gain an even greater understanding of Feng Shui gardening. Skip them, and you're still okay; you can still create a beautiful Feng Shui garden.

This icon is used to highlight Feng Shui principles being used to their fullest, most useful extent. If you pick only a few Feng Shui ideas to try, pick these.

Where to Go from Here

You don't have to read this entire book from start to finish. You won't hurt our feelings, honest. Well, maybe a little. But if you must skip around, here's how:

- If you're a Feng Shui novice, turn to Chapter 2 for basic information on the principles of Feng Shui.
- If you know a bit about Feng Shui but need a brush up on basic terms and concepts, turn to Chapter 3 to get your fill of chi, Bagua and yin/yang. (Hey, that sounds like a sandwich.)
- If your garden hasn't gotten off the ground yet, turn to Chapter 5 to guide you in the right direction (or the right eight directions, that is, there being eight important directions in Feng Shui).
- If you have an established garden and want to find out how to spiff it up the Feng Shui way, turn to Chapter 6 for the scoop.
- If you want to jump right into solving Feng Shui challenges in your garden, turn to Chapter 12.
- If you want to check out different ideas for designing a garden around a theme, turn to Part IV, which has chapters on everything from aromatherapy-herbal gardens to Zen gardens. (Or everything from A to Z.)

Part I

Planting the Seeds of Feng Shui: Principles of Feng Shui

"There are various schools of Feng Shui gardening. I aspire to the school of Feng Shui that wipes their feet before coming in from the outside."

In this part . . .

Feng Shui is about designing environments that make you (and your visitors) feel warm and welcome. You may know it's a kind of interior design, but it works on the outside, too. The garden is an environment that can definitely benefit from some Feng Shui savvy. The backyard is symbolic of your future, so take your future into your own hands!

In this part, we go over some of the basics of getting the energy moving in your garden. We give you the lowdown on the principles of Feng Shui and how they apply to the garden. We also tell you how to use a Feng Shui map to design your garden and improve the energy and abundance in it. And we go over how the power of intention works in Feng Shui.

Chapter 1

Digging into Feng Shui Gardening

In This Chapter

- Figuring out Feng Shui
- Dreaming up a Feng Shui garden
- Making your plan a reality

If you're not quite sure what Feng Shui is or how it can work in your garden, don't worry. We're here to make you fearless about Feng Shui.

In this chapter, we go over the principles of Feng Shui and tell you how to apply them to your garden to create a welcoming environment and much, much more. (Gee, do we sound like a late-night infomercial yet?)

Exploring Feng Shui Basics

Feng Shui, which is a Chinese design philosophy, means literally *wind and water.* In traditional Chinese beliefs, wind and water are the source of all life energy. This life energy, called *chi,* brings abundance and blessings into your environment and your life. So when you're designing according to the principles of Feng Shui, you're really encouraging the chi to flow into and throughout your space (not to mention your life).

The modern approach to Feng Shui that we use in this book is called *Black Hat sect,* and it combines traditional Feng Shui beliefs with Western approaches. While Eastern concepts, such as intuition, play a primary role, Western concepts, such as practicality, aren't overlooked. We discuss this further in Chapter 2.

Before you can get started on Feng Shui gardening, you need a roadmap to Feng Shui. No, Feng Shui isn't an actual physical location, but you get the idea. By following the guidelines we tell you about, you can plan a garden that not only feels friendly and welcoming, but that actually brings abundance into your life.

Grooving with chi and other Feng Shui principles

Feng Shui, the art of perfect placement, is about allowing life energy (chi) to move through your environment to bring harmony and balance. This good energy brings good stuff into your life.

To find perfect placement and encourage good chi flow, you need to use various Feng Shui principles. We discuss these principles in the following subsections.

In Chapter 3, we discuss in detail the Feng Shui concepts that you can't live without. Then, in Chapter 4, we help you tackle the challenge of getting living energy into your garden. We give you tips on how to keep the energy movin' and groovin'.

Raising the chi

The main goal in Feng Shui gardening is to raise the level of chi in the garden and make sure that it moves smoothly and freely throughout the space. In other words, you have to get rid of barriers to chi, and you need to use Feng Shui fixes (called *cures*) to raise the chi in areas where it may get trapped and stagnate.

You can also use cures to solve the problems that arise when chi moves too quickly through your garden. Chi moving too quickly doesn't do you (or your garden) any good, and can actually help create an unpleasant environment that's agitated instead of relaxed.

Applying the Bagua

The Bagua is your Feng Shui placement map. It symbolizes how your environment is connected to your life. The Bagua, which is shaped like an octagon, has nine Life Sectors that correspond with aspects of your own life. Those nine sectors are

- Career
- Knowledge
- Family

- Wealth
- Fame
- Relationships
- Children
- Helpful People
- T'ai Chi (overall health and well-being)

These Life Sectors have a physical location in your garden and a symbolic location in your life. All the Life Sectors should be present in your garden. If your garden is oddly shaped, one of the sectors may be "missing," which means that the corresponding area in your life will have problems. So if your oddly shaped garden is missing the Wealth sector, or what would be your Wealth sector is actually in the neighbor's backyard, you may find yourself losing money or just having "bad luck" — things don't go your way. See the section below, "Workin' it," for more information on placing the Bagua.

According to Feng Shui, enhancing the chi in a Life Sector in your garden increases abundance in that area of your life. So if you need a little more love in your life, make sure the Relationships sector gets the attention it needs. See Chapter 6 for more information about using the Bagua in your garden.

Incorporating the Five Elements

The Five Elements (those qualities that make up everything in the world — Earth, Metal, Water, Wood, and Fire) must all be present and in balance in a Feng Shui garden. The universe is made up of these elements working together, and you want to reflect that in your garden. The elements work together to create a harmonious, welcoming space. How the elements work together is called the *nourishing cycle* of the elements. More information about this can be found in Chapter 3.

However, you have to careful that you put the right elements together because sometimes the elements can cancel each other out. This is called the *controlling cycle* of the elements. For example, too much Water element can "put out" the Fire element, which leads to unbalance in the garden. For more information on using the elements wisely, see Chapters 3 and 6.

Balancing yin and yang energy

Yin/yang is the idea that life energy can have a passive and an active side. Yin/yang is based on a concept of the universe as containing complementary opposites — qualities that seem to be in contrast to each other but that actually work together. For example, soft and hard or light and dark are qualities that complement each other.

In Chapter 2, we show you how to keep passive and active energy (yin/yang) in balance, so that your garden doesn't make people frantic or put them to sleep.

Knowing the benefits of Feng Shui

Not a firm believer in mystical mumbo-jumbo? Well, Feng Shui isn't exactly mystical mumbo-jumbo, but you still may not believe in it. However, the beauty of Feng Shui is that you can apply it and benefit from it, even if you're a bit skeptical.

For instance, if you're not sure raising the chi in your environment can mean a corresponding improvement in your life, at least you'll agree that keeping the clutter down makes your garden more attractive. And paying attention to aesthetics, function, and design as you plan your garden makes your space more appealing and welcoming.

For more on how you can benefit from Feng Shui, see Chapter 4.

Planning Your Feng Shui Garden

Because a Feng Shui garden requires you to balance the Five Elements and pay attention to placement according to the Bagua, you need to think about what you're doing.

A Feng Shui garden doesn't happen by accident. In fact, in Feng Shui, your *intention* (your specific, conscious goal for why you're doing what you're doing) is the most important component. You have to know why you're doing something for it to make sense in a Feng Shui garden. Fortunately, doing something because you like it qualifies!

Choosing a function and a location for your garden

Before the first seed is planted, you can ensure that your garden blossoms with blessings. By having a specific plan and function for your garden (such as relaxation or entertainment) and picking the best location, you're already on the right track.

According to Feng Shui, certain locations are more favorable than others. A protected location is ideal for a garden. Also beneficial is a garden that isn't exposed to negative chi generated by nearby highways, tall buildings, and other threats.

Regular square and rectangular garden shapes are most *auspicious* (favorable) because you can easily use the Bagua to identify Life Sectors in such a garden. In an oddly-shaped garden, one of these symbolic Life Sectors may be missing. An oddly-shaped garden can also cause chi to move too quickly or get stuck and stagnate.

See Chapter 5 for more about possible functions and ideal locations for a Feng Shui garden.

Getting a theme going

Many people opt for theme gardens, and if that's your thing, you can create a theme garden that still adheres to Feng Shui principles.

You can choose a theme just because you like it *or* because your garden has certain limitations. For example, if you're living in cramped quarters and still yearn for a Feng Shui garden, we show you how to make the most of your space in Chapter 19, which is all about gardening in small areas.

You can choose your theme based on a certain function you have in mind for your garden. For example, if you want your garden to be a place of rest and relaxation, the Zen garden or the Taoist garden may appeal to you. Or perhaps you want your garden to stock your pantry. In that case, we recommend the kitchen garden or the aromatherapy-herbal garden.

You can also choose your theme based on the Feng Shui principle that inviting living energy into your garden can increase the abundance in your life. See the butterfly garden and the hummingbird garden if you're looking to raise the chi in a wonderfully Feng Shui way.

The following gardens work beautifully with Feng Shui:

- **Aromatherapy-herbal garden:** The smell of orange spices up the workday, while a bit of lavender helps you relax in the evening. Creating a garden that smells delicious and that can season your stew makes a lot of gardeners smile. In Chapter 13, we show you how to get started with an aromatherapy-herbal garden, and we show you how to do it Feng Shui style.

- **Hummingbird garden:** Got a thing for these feathered friends? In Chapter 14, we describe what you can do to bring hummingbirds into your garden year after year. We give you planting ideas and offer suggestions for keeping the hummingbirds happy — in a Feng Shui way.
- **Butterfly garden:** If you're a fancier of these flying beauties, a butterfly garden — which can serve as a new habitat and refuge for endangered butterfly species — is just the ticket. In Chapter 15, we show you which plants butterflies prefer, and we explain how to Feng Shui the butterfly garden.
- **Zen garden:** Enlightenment, anybody? If you'd like to get in touch with your inner being in the outer world, the calm and peaceful Zen garden may be the perfect choice for you. In Chapter 16, we describe how to create a traditional sand-and-stone garden and we also show how to adapt it to your own needs and interests. Zen gardens can be very Feng Shui.
- **Taoist garden:** Taoist philosophy says that nature is the greatest artist, and if you're inclined to agree, then a Taoist garden may be what you want. A Taoist garden focuses on the beauty of nature and how you can enhance it. In Chapter 17, we show you how to make a Taoist garden according to the principles of Feng Shui.
- **Kitchen garden:** Who wouldn't prefer a juicy red tomato ripe from her own garden compared to the pale and tasteless offerings of the supermarket? In Chapter 18, we describe how to create a vegetable patch to feed all your senses (and your tummy as well). We show you how to apply the principles of Feng Shui to the radishes (and the peppers, too!) in order to bring abundance into your life (and your kitchen).
- **Cramped quarters:** Okay, so cramped quarters may not really be a theme, but it is a special situation. And small-space gardens have a style and personality all their own.

  Many would-be gardeners think they can't do much to indulge their green thumbs, because they live in small spaces, rental properties, or other areas where the land available for planting is limited. Well, that's simply not true. You can plant a garden in a pile of pots. It may not be a large garden, but it can be functional and beautiful nonetheless. In Chapter 19, we give you pointers on creating a Feng Shui garden in a limited space — even something as small as a windowsill.

Making sure you have a plan that works for you

Most people are so busy with their lives, jobs, families, and other interests and activities that they're not sure they can keep up with a garden — and if they do make time to grow some flowers or veggies, they're not sure they have time to add Feng Shui to the mix.

Gardening doesn't have to be a time-consuming activity (but it certainly can be if you want it to). When planning and creating your Feng Shui garden, you need to keep in mind your needs, time, money, and interests. If you're short on time and cash, you shouldn't plan for a huge, elaborate garden. Beautiful doesn't equal extravagant.

In Chapter 9, we show how you can plan a garden designed to suit your needs.

Workin' it

Dreaming about your perfect garden is all well and good (and a great way to get motivated), but at some point you have to get down to brass tacks. We've found that the best way to do that is to sketch a layout of your garden and then apply the *Bagua* (the placement map) to figure out what's right and what's wrong. By placing the Bagua over the layout (with the Career sector oriented to the entrance to the garden), you can see which areas of the garden correspond with which Life Sectors. See Chapter 6 for more information on using the Bagua in the garden.

As we mention earlier in this chapter, each of the directions of the Bagua corresponds with a different part of your life (such as Family and Career). These Life Sectors should all be represented in your garden, and you can keep them vigorous and healthy with careful attention. The Five Elements should also be balanced in your garden.

Check out Chapter 6 for details on putting Feng Shui to work in your garden.

Carrying Out Your Plan

When carrying out your Feng Shui garden plan, you want to raise the chi and keep things in balance. This section discusses the key components of creating a Feng Shui garden full of abundance. We also provide a section at the end to clue you in on how to fix various Feng Shui problems that may crop up along the way.

Picking the right plants

Some plants are more Feng Shui than others. They give off good vibes. Some plants, such as roses, can be more problematic in a Feng Shui garden. You want to choose wisely when picking plants for your garden, making sure that you use Feng Shui-friendly plants whenever possible and using ones that are problematic with caution and care.

Plants with thorns and spikes may create negative or cutting chi, especially if they're planted where the thorns could catch on people's clothing or where the plants may seem subtly threatening to guests (for example, a hanging planter a person must walk under to get from one part of the garden to another). Plants with long, trailing vines can trip people up, so use them with care as well.

Friendlier plants include those with rounded leaves and blooms, especially plants that aren't aggressive in their growth.

You also want to choose color carefully, because some colors are more auspicious in certain locations. Chapter 10 provides the lowdown on picking plants for your Feng Shui garden.

Going au naturel

Don't worry; we're not telling you that you have to garden naked. (Although you can if you really want to.) What we mean is that according to the principles of Feng Shui, the natural way is the better way. Whenever possible, use natural materials and methods in your garden.

If you're wondering how to keep the toxic chemicals out of the garden without letting the caterpillars eat all your plants, flip to Chapter 7.

Inviting critters into your garden

Living critters create good vibes in a garden. They raise the chi, generate good living energy (usually), and otherwise make your garden appealing. So go ahead and invite those furry and feathered friends into your garden and treat them right. We show you how in Chapter 11.

In case you've got some critters that are doing more harm than good (the rabbits and squirrels refuse to leave your lettuce alone), we also show you how to discourage them in Chapter 11. Although all living energy is good energy, sometimes too much of a good thing is a bad thing.

Curing Feng Shui problems

Most Feng Shui problems have to do with the chi moving through the environment. Sometimes the energy is negative, such as when sharp angles from structures create cutting chi, or when plants with spikes or thorns are planted too close to places where visitors move about, catching on their clothes. Ugh. Sometimes chi gets stuck and stagnates. (Think of a pile of rotting weeds. Double ugh.) Chi can get stuck in dark corners and in spots where last year's leaves have drifted into a big pile. Sometimes the energy whizzes through the space so fast it doesn't have time to stop and lift your spirits, such as when yards and yards of wide-open prairie make up the garden with nothing to hold the chi in or encourage it to stop and stay awhile.

In any of these scenarios, you need to help the chi out — make the negative chi positive, speed up stagnating chi, and slow down chi that moves too fast.

In Chapter 12, we show you cures for these chi problems — everything from adding some lights to a dark corner to clearing the clutter in the gutters.

Seasoning your garden

A Feng Shui garden looks good throughout the year. Each season brings special surprises. As a Feng Shui gardener, you need to embrace what each season has to offer and make the most of it.

Even in the depth of winter, evergreens and bushes with bright berries can add color to your garden. You can also add ornaments, such as statues, that draw the eye when the leaves have fallen from the trees.

In Chapter 8, we show you how to keep your garden looking great all year long, and we also give planting suggestions to keep your flowers blooming from April to October.

Chapter 2

Laying the Groundwork for Feng Shui

In This Chapter

- Understanding Feng Shui
- Discovering the different types of Feng Shui
- Seeing Feng Shui design
- Creating auspicious placements

Applying the principles of Feng Shui to your garden helps you to create an environment you look forward to spending time in. Your garden can make you feel refreshed and rejuvenated — without investing in long hours of labor, lots of expensive parts, or hard-to-find artifacts.

In this book, we use the term *garden* loosely, to mean just about any patch of land situated near your home. We could be talking about an actual garden, or a front yard, side yard, or backyard — or a combination of any of the above.

Whether you're a beginning gardener or a veteran, Feng Shui can complement your urge to create beauty. Don't ever do something you don't like just because it's "good" Feng Shui. In fact, doing something you don't like is by definition "bad" Feng Shui. As you discover the principles of Feng Shui and figure out how to apply them to your garden, you use your own personal interests and preferences to create the perfect Feng Shui garden for your home.

Balance: The Essence of Feng Shui

Feng Shui, which is basically a design philosophy, is simply about placing objects (in this case, plants, lawn furniture, and related items) in an attractive, *auspicious* (beneficial) way. Your goal is to balance the various principles of Feng Shui to create a warm, welcoming space. You don't want any one element, principle or plant elbowing out all the others. Throughout the book, we show you how to develop this sense of balance.

I say Fung Shway, you say Feng Shway: Defining Feng Shui

Feng Shui literally means "wind and water." Wind and water, the two universal forces necessary for life, carry *chi* (or life energy or life force) throughout the world. Feng Shui harnesses this life energy to enrich your environment, bringing you abundance and balance. See Chapter 3 for more information on chi.

Through the auspicious or harmonious placement of design elements, Feng Shui brings blessings and balance into your life. This is the essence of Feng Shui; in fact, its purpose. If your environment harmonizes, then you feel comfortable and welcome there. If your environment is not in harmony, then you may feel uncomfortable and even subtly threatened on an energetic level.

You may not consciously think, "Gee, I'm feeling subtly threatened on an energetic level," but you may feel restless, overwhelmed, or otherwise out of sorts. Environments that make you want to take your toys and go home don't display good Feng Shui. Having such disharmony in your own environment makes it difficult for you to achieve the success in your life that you may hope to achieve.

Too much of any element creates disharmony in design, making your environment (and you) seem out of whack. Fortunately, Feng Shui doesn't throw up its hands in despair. Feng Shui has answers for you — *cures* (ideas for fixing Feng Shui problems) that can be used to correct the shortcomings in your environment (see Chapter 12).

Complementary opposites: Yin/yang in action

Taoist philosophy, an ancient Chinese way of looking at the universe, believes that simplicity and harmony create long life and good fortune. This philosophy is fundamental to Feng Shui. Many Taoist beliefs are integral to Feng Shui, including the concept of *yin/yang* (complimentary opposites). Taoist philosophy says that the universe is made up of conflicting, yet harmonious, elements.

Rather than being just opposites, these elements rely on each other for meaning. For example, night is meaningless without day, dark without light, hard without soft. Balancing these complementary opposites is an important part of Feng Shui. In other words, too much dark creates lack of balance as does too much or too little light.

Yin energy is associated with feminine qualities, darkness, rounded shapes, and passive energy. *Yang* energy is associated with masculine qualities, light, angular shapes, and active energy. Too much yin energy and you're yawning in no time; too much yang energy and your jangled nerves are screaming for a stay at a rest home. Check out Figure 2-1 for an illustration of the yin/yang symbol.

Figure 2-1: The yin/yang symbol shows how complementary opposites make up a whole.

See Table 2-1 for more yin/yang complementary opposites.

Table 2-1 Complementary Opposites: Yin/Yang

Yin	*Yang*
Feminine	Masculine
Cold	Hot
Night	Day
Quiet	Loud
Soft	Hard
Round	Sharp

In Feng Shui, balancing yin and yang qualities is essential. You can balance the two by carefully selecting colors, textures, shapes, and lighting. For example, a backyard with no shade, exposed to the full sun all day, has too much yang energy and is an uncomfortable environment. A backyard filled with towering oaks with no sunlight penetrating has the opposite problem — too much yin energy. Again, this creates an uncomfortable environment. Your mission, should you choose to accept it, is to create a nice balance between yin and yang energy. You want to create a garden that has some areas of shade, some areas of full sunlight, and some areas of transition — where, perhaps, the light is dappled.

And you need to consider the yin/yang energy as it presents itself throughout the year. Summer is naturally a more yang time of year, and lends itself to the creation of yin space for relief, perhaps by putting up a gazebo or garden tent. Winter is more naturally a yin time of year, and your garden could benefit from some living energy to stir things up (in other words, adopt a dog). Or add a bird feeder.

The fundamental principle of Feng Shui is to keep everything in balance.

Going Back to School: The Design Schools of Feng Shui

The earliest approaches to Feng Shui were based on Chinese numerology and astrology. According to legend, Feng Shui developed nearly 5,000 years ago during the reign of Emperor Fu Hsi (2900 B.C.). In the early stages, Feng Shui was primarily concerned with the best placement for graves, temples, and palaces. Over time, different approaches to Feng Shui developed into distinct styles called *schools.*

At one time, Feng Shui masters who shared the secrets of Feng Shui with people outside the imperial family could be put to death. Whew! Glad those days are gone, or we'd be in trouble.

Practically speaking: The Black Sect school

A recent arrival on the Feng Shui scene, Black Sect Tantric Buddhism school (if that's a mouthful, try Black Sect or Black Hat) is an approach to Feng Shui that combines principles of classical Feng Shui (see the "Where it all began: The Landform school" and "Which end is up? The Compass school" sections later in this chapter), Buddhism, Taoism, energy theory, and Western design concepts.

Grand Master Professor Thomas Lin Yun brought a form of the Black Sect school to the West from China over 35 years ago.

Black Sect Feng Shui features a practical, hands-on approach to Feng Shui that's very popular in the West. We follow this school in the book; it emphasizes concepts such as

- **Intention:** Stating what you want
- **The Mouth of Chi:** The position of entrances into an environment

Where it all began: The Landform school

Sometimes called the *Form school,* the Landform school is one of the oldest schools of Feng Shui that still has followers. Landform Feng Shui masters study the land itself to determine the best (most auspicious) locations for buildings. They take into consideration the forces of nature, including strong winds and erosion, note the symbolic shape of the land, and then calculate how the climate of the area combines with those natural features and formations to create a site either stable and auspicious or unstable and inauspicious. They also assess the energy or chi they feel in the land.

For example, if you live in a mountainous area, place your home with the back to the mountain to lend a feeling of stability. But if you place your house facing the mountain, you may feel a little hemmed in and slightly threatened.

Some Landform principles are used in Black Hat Feng Shui — such as considering the forces of nature when selecting a site — but other Landform principles are considered less important.

Which end is up? The Compass school

The *Compass school,* also an ancient approach to Feng Shui, relies on Chinese astrology to determine auspicious placement. The eight compass directions are particularly important. (Yes, eight directions; in addition to the four we know and love, Compass school includes northeast, northwest, southeast, and southwest.)

Your personal life directions, also known as your most favorable directions, are calculated using a special formula based on your birth year, and facing this direction is considered auspicious.

Spotting Feng Shui Design Elements

As you discover more about the principles of Feng Shui, you'll begin to observe them in action all around you. For example, you may notice the balance (or lack of balance) of yin/yang as you walk into a garden overgrown with trees that let in little light. Try to stay attuned to the principles and elements of Feng Shui in the world around you as you plan how to apply the principles to your own space.

The eyes have it: Developing Feng Shui eyes

As a practical matter, work to develop *Feng Shui eyes* — in other words, an appreciation for the concepts of Feng Shui design philosophy and an ability to spot Feng Shui elements when you see them (and to notice when you don't).

In Chapter 3, we go into further details about the principles and elements of Feng Shui. Use this information to spot Feng Shui (or lack of it) in gardens and nurseries you visit so you get a sense of what you want to do (and what you don't want to do).

Troubleshooting chi movement

In Feng Shui, *chi,* or life energy, needs to move freely through the environment. If it stagnates or gets stuck, the environment may become subtly unpleasant. In Chapter 3, we give you more information about chi and how it works, but keep in mind that making sure chi can move freely through your garden is a key to effective Feng Shui design.

But how does it feel? Relying on intuition

Inauspicious (bad) placement affects people on an energetic level. That is, you feel it but the feeling is pretty subtle. You can't always put a finger on what's troubling you about a certain space or environment.

What may be troubling you is poor design, according to Feng Shui. You may feel subtly threatened by certain types of plants, outdoor structures, and arrangements. Don't dismiss these feelings. Your intuition is an important part of Feng Shui. If something feels wrong, it is wrong. Try a different plant, a different placement, or a different arrangement.

Even better, work to understand your intuition. When you walk into an environment that makes you feel uncomfortable, try to understand why. Is it because the garden is cluttered with debris, dead leaves, and overgrown bushes? Is it because huge, out of proportion marble statues loom over you while you're trying to enjoy your tea? Being able to identify the source of your discomfort helps you avoid and eliminate Feng Shui mistakes.

While different people have different experiences — some people are creeped out by hanging plants while others love them — awareness of what your intuition is telling you helps you create a garden you love. Working to create a balance helps ensure that others will also find your garden attractive and welcoming.

Placing Plants Perfectly

Because your garden consists mainly of living things, Feng Shui in the garden emphasizes the selection and placement of plants of all types — shrubs, flowers, trees, and grasses. In this book, we also show you how to create gardens along a theme. Creating a theme garden requires special attention to the types of plants and other objects in your garden. See Chapters 13 through 18.

But unlike a pretty pot, plants don't always stay put, so take that into consideration as you plan. Know the plants that you're choosing. Understand how big they can grow, how aggressive they can be, and how soon they'll be blocking out the sun. (See Chapter 10)

Choose native plants for the way they fit perfectly into your garden and for the way they resist disease, drought, and bugs without pesticides, herbicides, or any other *cide.*

Planning an overall sense of well-being

A garden created according to the principles of Feng Shui is welcoming and friendly. You want to spend time there — and your friends do, too. Remember that the garden shouldn't just be picture-pretty, it should be a place where you can comfortably spend time. You should be able to stroll along the pathways and take a look at the pansies without fearing you may destroy the garden's perfect symmetry. In other words, don't just plan for looks, plan for use.

Creating harmony with natural materials

A cornerstone of Feng Shui is the use of natural materials whenever possible. Natural objects — whether plants, wood benches, mulch, or rock — are a treat to the senses. They're more visually appealing. And because they're natural, they fit better into the garden environment. In other words, think twice about purple plastic lawn furniture, no matter how cheap it is.

Chapter 3

Feng Shui's Balancing Act

In This Chapter

- Moving chi
- Envisioning the Elements
- Betting on the Bagua

In Chapter 2, we talk about balancing the different passive and active energies of *yin/yang* (complementary opposites). While creating this balance is essential, Feng Shui includes other concepts that *also* have to be balanced with one another. If this sounds like too much of a balancing act for you to undertake, consider the rewards: Understanding how these concepts work together can help you create good Feng Shui in your garden. And creating good Feng Shui in your garden can help you create not just the garden of your dreams but also the life of your dreams! Feng Shui is thought to actually affect your life by affecting your environment. In other words, bringing abundance into your garden can bring abundance into your life.

In this chapter, we reveal the ancient Chinese secrets that make up the foundation of Feng Shui. But wait! Don't touch that dial. It's not as complicated as it may sound. Really.

Flowing Like a River: The Movement of Chi

Chi, or life energy, flows through the universe (it also flows through you and me). According to Feng Shui, everything in the natural world around us contains chi — including the land and sky.

Chi moves through our environment (such as our gardens) like wind or water might. (Hmm, maybe that's where Feng Shui gets its name: Feng Shui *means* "wind and water.") When chi moves freely throughout a space, it creates a positive feeling — good vibes, you might say.

Chi, Wally, what's that for?

If you want chi to bring all of its abundant blessings to your garden, it must flow freely and smoothly through your environment. If the chi is blocked and can't get through, it creates stagnant or negative energy in an area. If the chi gets stuck — swirling around in a corner instead of flowing through the space, for instance — it can depress the energy in your environment.

The garden in Figure 3-1, with its rounded paths, varying heights of plants, and interesting objects, is an example of good chi flow through a garden.

Photo courtesy of author

Figure 3-1: Chi moves freely in this garden.

An essential part of creating good Feng Shui in a garden is to make certain that chi can flow freely and smoothly throughout the space. When chi runs into problems, those problems can be fixed with *cures* — objects that raise the chi and create good energy. Examples include objects such as water fountains and wind chimes. See Chapter 12 for more information on cures.

But what can it do for me?

Harnessing chi enriches your environment and creates balance in your life. Chi that flows freely and smoothly in your environment brings abundance and blessings to you.

Want more? Well, okay. Cultivating chi creates good energy that can make you feel more energized. It can help you achieve more in your personal or career life.

More? Good chi makes a space feel warm and welcoming; it helps you create spaces where you *want* to be. And it doesn't even cost a dime (although we're happy to take contributions on behalf of chi).

Chi in your garden increases abundance. So, if your tomatoes look a little puny, maybe all they need is some good chi coming their way. A garden with free-flowing chi is attractive and welcoming to visitors — and to you.

Elementary, My Dear Watson: The Five Elements of Feng Shui

According to Feng Shui, everything in the world consists of one of the *Five Elements*. These elements are

- Earth
- Metal
- Water
- Fire
- Wood

In Feng Shui, inviting all Five Elements into your garden is crucial to good design and placement. Each element symbolizes an aspect of the universe and the world around you. Keeping the Five Elements balanced in your garden raises the chi, keeping it moving happily and energetically throughout the place.

If any one of the elements gets out of balance, it can tip the chi in your garden out of balance, too. For example, too much Water element can depress the energy (chi) in your garden and even make you feel like you're drowning!

Spotting an out-of-whack element takes practice. A good place to start is to recognize how each of the elements is represented in the garden. Then you can see if you have too much of one element and not enough of another. For instance, plants represent the Wood element. If your garden consists only of plants and no other objects, such as a water fountain or a stone bench, then the Wood element is probably too dominant in your garden.

Each element has a *yin* (passive) and *yang* (active) side (also called an *aspect*). Water lapping at the shore on a tranquil summer's day is yin. Water pounding against the docks during a storm is yang.

Ideally, you keep the Five Elements balanced with each other while keeping their yin and yang aspects also in balance. In other words, you want your surroundings to contain all Five Elements, but not all Five Elements in their yang aspect. Surrounding yourself with balanced elemental energy is a better plan. When you're in a place that symbolizes the special kind of energy each element produces, you feel comfortable and your environment is in harmony with the universe. That's a good thing! See the section, "Making the Five Elements work together" for more on balancing the Five Elements.

Making the Five Elements work together

If all the Five Elements are represented in a space, and none of the elements dominates, you create a feeling of comfort and harmony.

You can represent each element either literally or symbolically. Each element has colors and shapes associated with it, and you can use these colors and shapes to symbolically represent the element (see Table 3-1). Each element also has certain objects and compass directions associated with it. For example, Wood element can be literally represented with wooden objects and symbolically represented with color (greens and blues), shape (rectangle), objects (plants and flowers), and compass direction (east).

Table 3-1 Elementary Characteristics of the Five Elements

Element	*Associated Colors*	*Applicable Objects*	*Direction*	*Special Shape*
Wood	Greens and blues	Plants and flowers	East	Rectangle
Fire	Reds	Lightning, candles, sunlight, and fireplaces	South	Flame and triangle
Earth	Yellows and earth tones	Soil, ceramic tile, and brick	Southwest and northeast	Square
Metal	White, gray, and pastel colors	Metal	West	Circle
Water	Black and dark colors	Water features, glass, and crystals	North	Freeform irregular shapes

How the Five Elements work together is an essential principle of Feng Shui. The Five Elements relate according to two symbolic cycles — nourishing and controlling — neither of which is better than the other. Each element goes through both cycles. The cycles simply show how the elements relate to each other. You can use them to create balance in your garden by visualizing the relationship between the elements. See Figure 3-2 for a representation of these two cycles.

The nourishing cycle

Here's how the nourishing cycle works:

- Wood feeds Fire
- Fire makes Earth
- Earth creates Metal
- Metal holds Water
- Water nurtures Wood

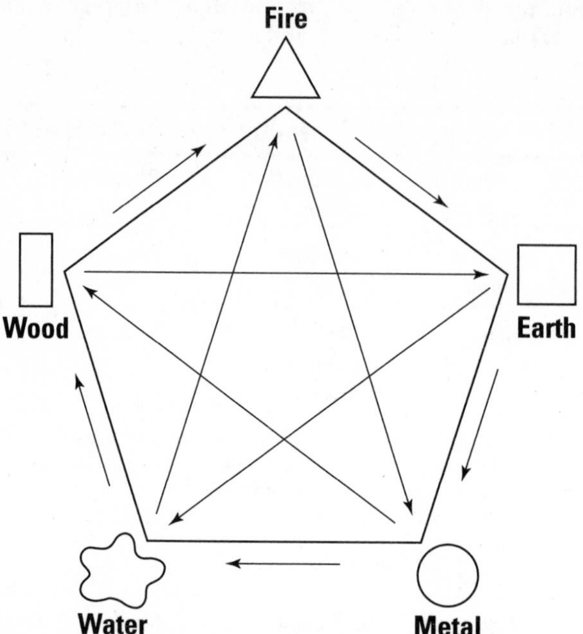

Figure 3-2: In the nourishing cycle, the elements enhance one another; in the controlling cycle, they diminish one another.

In other words, if you put a log into a fire, you feed the fire. Fire creates ashes, or Earth, out of the log. Earth creates Metal (the ore you can find if you dig deep enough), and Metal (in the shape of a container) holds Water, and Water helps Wood (plant material) grow.

In practical terms, you can use the nourishing cycle to balance the elements in your garden. For example, suppose you glance around and notice that you have very little Metal element in your garden. For aesthetic and practical reasons you don't want to add metal furniture to your patio (it can be ugly and it rusts). To solve this dilemma, you add Earth element in the form of ceramic pots and stone tiles. Because Earth creates Metal, adding the Earth element also symbolically creates more Metal element in your garden.

The controlling cycle

Here's how the controlling cycle works:

- Wood consumes Earth
- Earth blocks Water

- Water extinguishes Fire
- Fire melts Metal
- Metal cuts Wood

In other words, plants (Wood) use up Earth as they grow. Earth (think of a dam) prevents Water from moving freely. A bucket of Water puts out a Fire; a bit of Metal placed in Fire melts. A metal axe cuts wood.

The controlling cycle shows how you can tame a dominant element. For example, suppose you have too much Wood in your garden. You can take away some of the Wood, or you can add Metal, which symbolically cuts Wood, to reduce the effect of the Wood element and to help create more balance in your garden.

Balancing the Five Elements in your garden

Balancing the Five Elements creates a feeling of harmony and welcome in your garden. Because plants represent the Wood element, and you have a lot of plants in your garden (just guessing), you need to be especially careful to balance the Wood element with the other four elements. In other words, don't drag more Wood into the garden (literally *or* symbolically). Instead, consider how to pull the other elements in.

See Table 3-2 for the different objects and materials you often find in a garden and how they're associated with the Five Elements.

Table 3-2 Elements and the Material World

Element	*Objects and Materials*
Wood	Bamboo, wicker, and natural fabrics (such as cotton)
Earth	Clay, terra cotta, ceramic, and stone (granite or marble)
Metal	Metal fixtures and wrought iron
Water	Ponds, fountains, glass, crystal, and mirrors
Fire	Fire (grill, firepit), candles, tiki torches, and outdoor lighting

Avoiding too much of a good thing

We warned you that too much of one of the Five Elements was not a good thing. Take a look at Table 3-3 to see why. An element in balance is *good,* an element slightly out of balance can create difficulties — the *bad,* and an element completely out of whack can create big problems — the *ugly.*

Table 3-3 Element Overload

Element	*The Good*	*The Bad*	*The Ugly*
Wood	Enhances flexibility and creativity	A little rigid	Extreme idealism
Earth	Grounds you	Makes you a bit cautious	Terrified of taking risks
Metal	I've got the power	Unwilling to compromise	Aggression, argumentative
Water	Renews and relaxes you	Makes you feel wishy-washy	Help! I'm drowning!
Fire	Invigorating	Overstimulated	Type A, anyone? Confrontational

Your Cat's Not the Only One with Nine Lives: The Life Sectors

In Feng Shui, different types of energy come from each of the eight directions (north, northeast, northwest, south, southeast, southwest, east, west). Each direction has different characteristics associated with it and is also associated with a specific aspect of your life. Each direction equals one *Life Sector,* or area that symbolizes a part of your life. Because the center also counts as a Life Sector, a total of nine Life Sectors affect what happens in your life.

Bagua your pardon? What's a Bagua?

An eight-sided figure, called the *Bagua* (ba-gwa), symbolizes the eight directions and nine Life Sectors. The Bagua, also called

Pa-kua or *Feng Shui Octagon,* encompasses all the principles, tying them together in a neat little package. Check out Figure 3-3 for a sample.

The Bagua helps you identify the various Life Sectors in your garden — sort of like a map. It shows you how to raise the chi in various parts of the garden — and also raise the chi in various parts of your life! See Chapter 6 for more information on the practical uses of the Bagua in the garden.

The Nine Life Sectors of the Bagua are:

- Fame
- Relationships
- Children
- Helpful People
- Career
- Knowledge
- Family
- Wealth
- Overall Health and Well-being

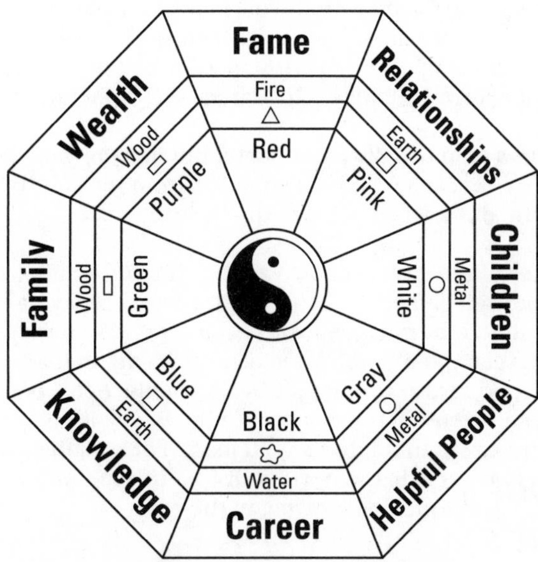

Figure 3-3: The Bagua is your garden's roadmap.

Table 3-4 shows how the Bagua and the Five Elements are linked.

Table 3-4 Elementary Bagua

Bagua Direction	*Element*	*Symbolizes*
East, southeast	Wood	Growth, new ideas
West, northwest	Metal	Strength, action
Northeast, southwest	Earth	Nurturing, production
South	Fire	Enthusiasm, completion
North	Water	Contemplation

Mapping it out

The Bagua is like a map of your space. If you place the Bagua over an area (figuratively speaking), you can see where the various Life Sectors fall in your space. Why is this important? Well, because you want to have good things happen in your life. If you enhance the chi in a Life Sector in your garden, you're enhancing the chi in the corresponding part of your life. What's not to like?

You position the Bagua with the entrance to a space corresponding with the north, or Career sector. If no entrance exists (you're using the Bagua in the middle of a cornfield — okay, maybe not a common occurrence), place the Career sector facing north.

The top of a map usually faces north, but in Feng Shui, it faces south! Why? Because the best chi flows from the south. Be aware of this little quirk when you use the Bagua.

The center of the Bagua, known as the *T'ai Chi,* symbolizes overall health and well-being. The other eight sectors are equally important and should be balanced with each other. None is given more emphasis than the others. When all sectors are in harmony, the result is good health and happiness. To achieve this harmony, you need to pay attention to each part of the Bagua in the garden, not just the areas that interest you most. For example, your prize begonias may grow in the north, but that doesn't mean you should neglect the watermelons growing in the east.

Using a Bagua

You can apply the Bagua to your own garden to ensure that the Life Sectors are balanced and so enhance the chi in any sector that could use a boost. Love life lacking? The Relationship sector needs your attention!

Here's what to do:

1. **Decide how you're going to approach the Feng Shui process.** Do you want to Feng Shui the front yard first, then the back yard next year? Or only the front yard? Or only the backyard? Or the entire lot together in one glorious Feng Shui frenzy?
2. **Sketch a plan of your garden (whether front yard, back yard, or both).** If sketching the entire lot, show where your house is in relationship (and in proportion) to the yards.
3. **Indicate any structures that aren't going anywhere soon.** For instance, utility poles and electrical boxes.
4. **Place a template of the Bagua (see Figure 3-3) over the plan of your garden to see where the Life Sectors fall.**

If you're applying the Bagua to your:

- **Front yard:** Position the Career sector facing the entrance to the space; generally the street.
- **Back yard:** Position the Career sector facing the main entrance to the yard, either the back door to your house or the main gate.
- **Entire lot:** Position your house in the center and the Career sector facing mouth of chi or welcoming energy (of the driveway or entrance to the property).

The Bagua is an octagon and fits most neatly over a square-shaped space. However, you can manipulate the Bagua (squishing it together, pulling it out a bit) to make it fit your lot plan a bit better. See Figure 3-4.

The most auspicious lot is a regular shaped square or rectangle. If your yard is unevenly shaped, a portion of the Bagua may actually be missing — a serious problem in Feng Shui terms. You need to use your creativity to fix this problem, and maybe get the number of a good Feng Shui consultant. (See Chapter 4 for more on curing Feng Shui problems that ail your garden.)

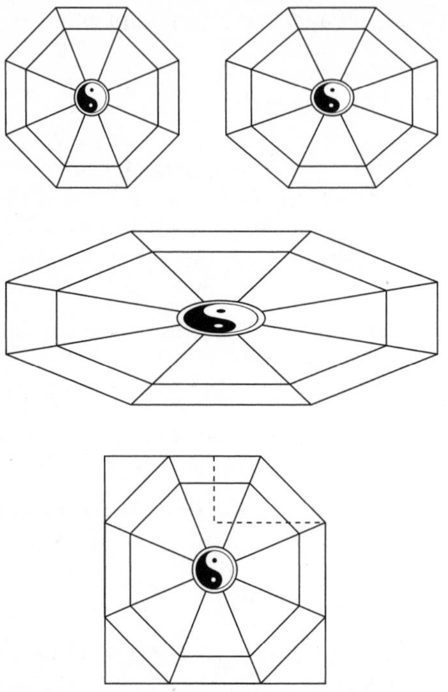

Figure 3-4: You can manipulate the Bagua to make it fit over any square or rectangular garden.

Raising the chi in a Life Sector

If you want to make changes in certain areas of your life — for example, you're thinking your Wealth sector could use some attention — you can *raise the chi* in that sector, which means you enhance the energy in that sector. You can do this by adding cures (see Chapter 4), or by adding more of the element or color associated with that sector.

For example, Wealth is associated with the color purple and with the Wood element. Fortunately, Wood is easy to come by in a garden (plants, trees, shrubs). You can even plant some purple pansies in the Wealth Sector for a double-dose of chi-enhancing cures.

See Table 3-5 to see how to understand the Life Sectors in the garden.

Table 3-5 The Bagua in the Garden

Direction	*Sector*	*Best Use of the Sector*
South	Fame	Entertainment, bolstering your standing in the community.
Southwest	Relationships	Gardening. Add a bench big enough for two and a gazing ball in hot pink.
West	Children/Creativity	Play area for children, creative gardening
Northwest	Helpful People/Travel	Entertainment could go here (dear friends and clients). Add wind chimes, symbolizing the friends in your life, a gate or portal symbolizing entry into adventure and faraway places.
North	Career	A water feature, such as pond or fountain. Add a bed of deep blue flowers. Iris is particularly good.
Northeast	Knowledge	A bench or swing for peaceful reading or contemplation. Play would not be a good choice for this sector.
East	Family	Play and active sports, especially in terms of family get-togethers where playful activities are part of the festivities. Add healthy plant life (Wood element), a memento of your parents mounted on the back of a bench or in stepping stones; their names carved on a rock.
Southeast	Wealth	A purple gazing ball, metal bell, or bowl or object you love raises the chi. Fountains are good here (Water Element feeds Wood Element).
Center	T'ai Chi	Great for a garden. Not so good for a fountain because Water erodes Earth.

Nine Life Sectors or eight?

We say that the Bagua has nine Life Sectors that correspond with various aspects of your life. But does the Bagua have nine Life Sectors, or does it have eight? Well . . . both.

In Black Hat Sect Feng Shui, which is what we describe in this book, only 8 life sectors exist, which correlate with the eight trigrams of the I-Ching, an ancient Chinese book of wisdom. Compass School Feng Shui teaches this as well, calling the eight life sectors the Eight Mansions.

The center of the Bagua, called the Ming Tang or the T'ai Chi, receives energies from all the surrounding sectors and is represented by the earth element. To avoid confusion and to make the Bagua easier to understand, we call this the ninth Life Sector. The T'ai Chi is associated with your overall health and well-being, although some Feng Shui practitioners place health in the Family sector. So the ninth life sector has special properties. . . including the property of not being a life sector at all, depending on how you look at it!

The Bagua compass directions are used in a symbolic way in this book. In other words, the Career sector, which is sometimes called the North sector, doesn't always literally face the North. It faces the entrance to your space — whether that space is a garden or a home office. Here's a quick translation for what the symbolic compass directions correspond to, as if you were standing at the entrance and looking into the space:

- **Career sector:** north = entrance or front
- **Knowledge sector:** northeast = front left
- **Family sector:** east = left side
- **Wealth sector:** southeast = rear left
- **Fame sector:** south = rear
- **Relationships sector:** southwest = rear right
- **Children sector:** west = right side
- **Helpful People sector:** northwest = front right
- **T'ai Chi sector:** center = center

Chapter 4

Designing Your Garden to Attract Good Chi

In This Chapter

- Raising your life energy through a Feng Shui garden
- Creating garden entrances that welcome chi
- Using pathways, corners, and plants to encourage chi flow
- Balancing yin/yang energy to maintain chi flow

A purposefully planned Feng Shui garden can help you achieve prosperity, harmony, and balance in your life. What's not to like? Fundamentally, Feng Shui is about creating spaces that are comfortable and welcoming to you and your guests — so even if you're not entirely convinced that putting goldfish in your pond can improve your life, designing your garden according to the principles of Feng Shui still makes it an attractive, enjoyable place.

In this chapter, we give you some reasons why you may want to Feng Shui your garden, and we also give you tips and techniques for bringing *chi* — life energy — into your space.

Why Should I Feng Shui My Garden?

Jayme Barrett, Feng Shui consultant and one of the contributors to this book, says, "Your garden is an extension of your home." Raising the *chi,* or life energy, outside your house encourages the chi to flow through your house. A beautiful garden creates good chi that comes in through the windows and doors of your home, so even when you're not out in the garden, the garden affects you.

Having good chi-flow through your space makes you feel more comfortable and even happier. It brings positive energy to you, making you feel more upbeat and positive. Negative energy, on the other hand, can make you feel stuck and depressed.

See Chapter 2 for more info on chi.

Achieving your goals through intentions

Creating a Feng Shui garden is a way to manifest intentions for your life. An *intention* is a purpose or goal — the reason you're doing what you're doing. Whether you want a good relationship with your parents or a better job, a Feng Shui garden is a means for getting what you want — meeting your goals and dreams. What do you want from your life, personally and professionally? In your garden, you can design an environment that moves you closer to those dreams. Ours happen to include Brad Pitt, but yours may vary.

Ask yourself what your dream is — what you want in your life — and how you can represent that in your garden. Placing objects and scenery that symbolize your dreams can help you make them a reality. For example, if you feel lonely and want to set a goal (create an intention) to change that, you can design a garden that encourages social gatherings. (You didn't really think we could guarantee Brad Pitt, did you?)

Use your imagination as you think about what you can achieve in your garden. Jayme suggests, "If you've always wanted to live in Italy, then get Italian gardening books. If you like the Tuscan vineyard feeling, how can you create a baby vineyard?" In other words, even though Arizona doesn't have oceanfront property, you can create the impression that it does!

See Figure 4-1 for an example of a Tuscan Villa in the Midwest!

Even skeptics can benefit

You don't have to be an ardent believer in the principles of Feng Shui to benefit from the practice. Even if you're not quite convinced that raising the chi in the Career sector can help your career, paying attention to design and balance in your garden can produce a pleasant outdoor environment where you and your guests enjoy spending time.

But we're so sure Feng Shui will work for you . . . no, wait, that's Ginsu knives. But trust us. Feng Shui *does* work.

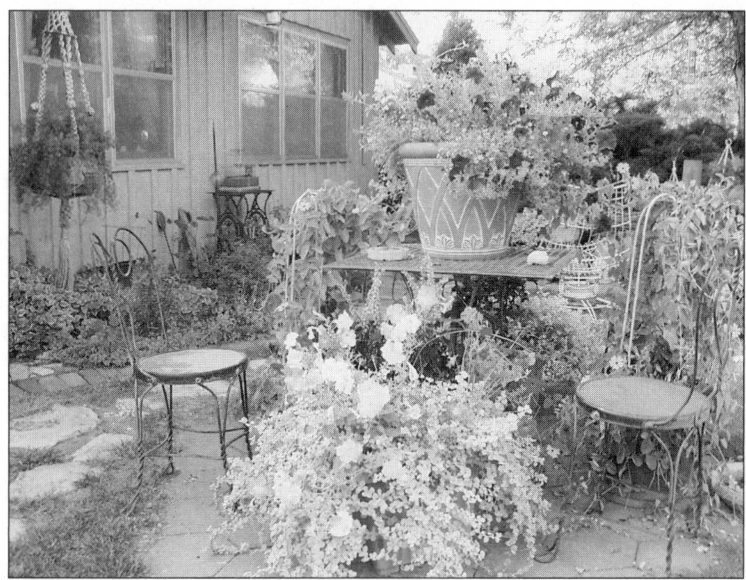

Photo courtesy of author

Figure 4-1: The Tuscan Villa Look in Dodge City, Kansas.

Inviting Chi into Your Garden

Got chi? Feng Shui is all about bringing chi into your life, your yard, and your home. With the right garden design, you can create vibrant, positive energy that stimulates you, welcomes you, energizes, or relaxes you — depending on what you need. Good life energy certainly beats negative, depressing energy. (You know your friend who's down all the time, no matter what good stuff happens? Way too much negative chi there. Hang a wind chime around her neck and see if matters improve.)

Where should you concentrate your gardening energies? According to the principles of Feng Shui, the backyard represents your future, so working on the backyard before worrying about other areas of your lot makes sense. (And if you don't have a backyard . . . uh-oh. Time to call up your real estate agent. Just kidding!)

Inviting chi into your garden and convincing it to stay (without it rushing over to the neighbor's house) is the main work you have ahead of you. Think of chi as a big dog that'll bolt out the front door if you're not careful. (Or through the window, or down the back steps.) It can be trained, but you have to know how to do it.

Opening the Mouth of Chi: Entrances to your garden

Chi comes into your garden through the entrance, known as *the Mouth of Chi*. If you have a gate, chi comes through that way. If your house has a backdoor that opens to the garden, chi enters that way. See Figure 4-2 for an example of the Mouth of Chi.

If your garden has more than one entrance, the main entrance is the most important when you're considering how chi enters your garden. The main entrance is simply the gate or door you (and your family and guests) use most often to get into the yard.

The chi that enters your garden can bring positive or negative energy with it, depending on what's happening outside the entrance. You want to welcome the positive chi and discourage the negative chi.

Photo courtesy of author

Figure 4-2: This decorative gate is the Mouth of Chi, allowing chi (and people!) to enter the garden.

For example, if your garden entrance faces an inauspicious building, such as a hospital, the hospital can create negative, depressing chi, which can enter your garden. To prevent this, hang a Bagua mirror (a special outdoor mirror shaped like an octagon) to deflect the negative energy. See Chapter 5 for more information on preventing negative energy from entering your garden.

The entrance to your garden lets in people as well as chi. An inviting, well-kept entrance reflects well on you; a dirty, cluttered, unattractive entrance — well, let's not go there.

For best Feng Shui results, limit the number of entrances to your garden. This gives you more control over how the chi enters and moves through your garden. Make your entrance (or entrances) attractive and interesting (see Chapter 5). Our friendly landscape architect Herb Schaal says, "The walk to an entrance — whether to a garden or through the front yard to the front door of the house — should be rich in experiences. Too many entrances are designed liked you'd find in an army barracks." Check out Figure 4-3 for an enticing front entrance.

Photo courtesy of author

Figure 4-3: This entrance invites people in.

Deflecting bad chi at entrances

Negative chi, sometimes called *cutting chi,* goes by the name of *sha chi* in Feng Shui. If something outside your garden entrance creates sha chi and sends it into your garden, you need to take action! The following can create negative chi, especially when aimed at entrances:

- High-tension power lines
- Sharp corners of buildings
- Large, overpowering buildings
- Cemeteries, hospitals, and police or fire stations
- Dead ends

You can counteract the effects of these ills by moving. No, no, just joking. You don't need to do anything that drastic. To help deflect negative energy and raise the good chi, try placing any of the following just outside the entrance:

- Wind chimes
- Victorian gazing balls
- Upward lighting (walkway lighting that projects up)
- "Guardian" or protective statues, like fu dogs

See Chapter 12 for more information on cures for negative chi.

Encouraging good chi at entrances

Chi is by nature positive and beneficial; only under certain conditions does it become negative and cutting. So in the absence of negative chi, you have positive chi! In other words, all chi is positive until proven guilty. If you want to ensure that the chi entering your garden is good chi, you can always raise the chi in the area by adding cures near the front entrance — wind chimes, water fountains, and more. See Chapter 12 for further information on cures. You can also keep the area neat and uncluttered — sweep up those autumn leaves before spring! Neatness helps beneficial chi flow into your garden.

Opening the Moon Gate: Doors, gates, and archways

Archways and *Moon Gates* (open spaces in a wall) throughout the garden (not just at the entrance) help create a welcoming garden setting. Framing part of the garden with an archway or moon gate invites the eye to see what's beyond. It also invites the chi to move along into the space.

For chi to move freely through your garden, you need to avoid solid doors and entrances to your garden. If your garden or yard is fenced, make sure that spaces are between the boards or the links to allow the chi to come through. If the main entrance is the backdoor to your house, add a screen door and keep the main door open when possible to allow chi to circulate.

Here are a few other points to keep in mind:

- A short gate (waist high) allows more chi to move into the garden.
- A tall gate slows chi down.
- A brightly painted gate — red or orange — stimulates the chi.
- A blue or green gate slows the chi a bit.

Fixing wide-open spaces

Chi doesn't flow smoothly and freely in wide-open spaces. It just sits there and then goes away after a while. Under certain conditions, it can also collect and stagnate, creating unhealthy, negative chi. So if your landscape is flatter than a pancake, you need to do some work to raise the level of chi.

To break up wide-open spaces, create different levels in your garden. Consider the following suggestions:

- A wooden deck elevates a portion of the environment.
- Raised flowerbeds also interrupt a wide-open space.
- Adding large boulders can create yang energy to counteract the yin energy of wide, open flat spaces. You can get large boulders at rock garden supply stores, some nurseries, the occasional quarry, and, depending on where you live, your own backyard. See Figure 4-4.
- Add a backing to the space — for instance, a wall, lattice, or trees.

Photo courtesy of author

Figure 4-4: Adding boulders breaks up this otherwise empty space.

No, chi, don't leave so soon!

Entrances invite chi into your garden, but that doesn't mean it stays there. As mentioned in the "Fixing wide-open spaces" section, flat, open areas allow chi to dissipate. Other problems, such as the following, can also cause chi to leave an area.

- A fence that's taller than the house can trap the chi so that it doesn't move freely.
- Land that drops away sharply can cause the chi to drop away sharply too — instead of moving freely and smoothly throughout the space.
- Fences, walls, or trees that are too close to the house can also trap the chi so that it doesn't move smoothly and freely but instead collects and stagnates. This can also seem subtly threatening to the inhabitants of the house.
- A garden that's exposed at the top of a hill with no fences or buildings to offer protection from the elements doesn't encourage chi to stay. The chi moves away from this space very quickly.

If you have a very flat space or a yard that slopes sharply or drops off, adding a "backing" to the space can help — a wall, lattice, or trees — so that the chi doesn't leave the yard.

Moving Chi Through Your Garden

You've invited chi into your garden by creating an appealing entrance. You have a nicely terraced yard — already fenced in so that the chi doesn't just run off. Now what? You don't want the chi to sit down and stay for a while — you want it to mingle and circulate, just like a good party guest.

Clearing the clutter

An important step in moving chi through your garden is to clear the clutter. Obstacles that get in the way of flowing chi include overgrown plants, cluttered landscapes, and dead and dying plants. Dead and dying plants symbolize dead and dying chi — exactly what you don't want! Such plants depress the whole environment. Plant thriving new ones instead.

When you plant, keep in mind that overcrowding is another obstacle for chi. You want to see the individual plants and flowers in your garden. Alternate empty space with full space to create a nice yin/yang balance. Not every spare inch of ground has to be jammed with flowers. Give yourself the chance to admire and see the beauty of each plant in its setting. Remember that being in your garden should make you feel motivated and inspired, not overworked and frustrated.

You can also add cures, such as lighting and *living energy* (the energy created by living creatures) to raise the chi in your garden. (Chapter 11 is all about inviting living energy into your garden; Chapter 12 discusses Feng Shui cures in detail).

Cornering chi

Avoid leaving corners of the yard or garden empty. Leaving the corners empty can cause the chi to stagnate, especially if the corner is fenced (which may trap the chi). Add flowers, a water feature, or lighting to help energize the corners.

Planting a tree or placing another sturdy feature (such as a large boulder or a statue) in the corner can help anchor and protect the area so that the energy doesn't dissipate. Container plants work well for a quick cure.

Parading chi down pathways

Pathways allow you to guide the chi throughout your garden. They can lead chi to corners it would otherwise avoid. They can also invite guests to wander through the garden and partake of all its delights!

Straight paths can speed chi up and curving paths can slow it down. You may use one or the other depending on whether you're trying to invite active or passive energy into a certain part of the garden.

Staying off the straight and narrow

A straight pathway, especially one that leads right to an entrance or door, can create rushing energy. Because the chi moves too fast, a poison arrow effect is produced with the poison arrow stabbing right at the entrance. As the phrase "poison arrow" suggests, this isn't a good thing.

Avoid placing too many straight paths and right angles in your yard and garden. If you already have straight pathways, change some of them to curved pathways. Planting bushy shrubs along the pathway also helps keep the chi from barreling down it.

The occasional use of a straight path can raise the chi but only in the right place. If part of your garden has very passive, yin energy, a straight path leading to it can generate some yang, active chi. You may be able to feel this depressed energy. Also, be aware that dark areas are more likely to have passive energy.

Creating curves

Curving paths tend to make for better Feng Shui. Such paths encourage the chi to move gently and easily throughout the space. They also make for a pleasant walk for you and your guests, inviting visitors to experience and see the entire garden.

You can make paths out of different materials. Natural materials are preferred, and rock and mulch are good choices. When selecting your materials, keep in mind the balance of the elements (see Chapter 3 for more on the Five Elements). Mulch, for example, is a

Wood element, and most gardens have an abundance of Wood. So instead of creating an imbalance by using too much Wood element in your garden, choose rock or pea gravel, which represent the Earth element. Using rock to construct your paths can help balance out the elemental energy.

You can use bricks, paving stones, and blocks of various materials to pave a pathway. Most of these pavers are made from stone, and they also represent the Earth element.

Try making some pathways out of grass. You can edge a grass pathway with flowers to lead visitors (and chi) from one part of the garden to another.

Remembering that paths run two ways

Don't forget that paths run two ways — to and from. Sometimes you may focus, for example, on how a path leads from the house to the garden without also remembering that it leads from the garden to the house. (That almost sounds profound, doesn't it?)

Chi runs along the path in both directions, so consider the impact of sending chi in both directions. In other words, if you step out from your back door and a straight pathway leads to an area of passive, yin energy, you may think that's fine, as areas of passive energy can use faster-moving yang energy. But if you turn around, you see that the straight path also leads directly to your back door, which means that lots of yang energy may be rushing towards your house. That may not be what you want.

Also, remember that visitors walk along the path in both directions, so make the experience pleasing from either direction.

Keeping the Chi Coming

In addition to using pathways to move chi throughout the garden, remember to apply the concept of yin/yang. Balancing active and passive energy keeps the chi moving smoothly and freely throughout your space. Don't let one type of energy dominate. Instead, keep them in balance. For example, the pathways that run throughout the garden produce yang energy. You can balance the yang created by these paths with grassy areas or by lining the paths with plants, which create yin energy. See Chapter 2 for more information on yin/yang.

Be creative in balancing yin/yang. Try the following:

- Balance flat land with raised beds, terraces, or decks.
- Create areas of sunlight and shade.
- Make sure you have flowering plants mixed with foliage plants.
- Plan various heights: ground, shrubs, and trees.
- Put shells or pebbles in a water element to balance hard and soft.

Streams can help move chi through your garden. Consider installing a larger pond and creating a small stream that flows from it into a smaller pond. Adding small footbridges over a pond or connecting one area of the garden to another also moves chi throughout your garden.

Part II

Getting Started on Your Feng Shui Garden

"I used an all natural method of pest control, but we're still getting an occasional vacuum cleaner salesman in the garden."

In this part . . .

Break out your dream plans and landscape photos, and get ready to grow the garden of your dreams. In this part, we lead you step by step through the process of creating a Feng Shui garden. We not only give you tips on planning a garden from scratch but also give you pointers for bringing the principles of Feng Shui into an already-established garden. We show you how to identify the functions of your garden, how to establish it in the right place, and how to bring the most blessings into your garden — and into your life! We give you the dirt on gardening naturally, creating a garden that delights in all seasons, and planning a garden that fits your gardening interests and needs — all according to Feng Shui design.

Chapter 5

Designing the Garden of Your Dreams

In This Chapter

- Deciding on your garden's purpose
- Choosing the location
- Understanding the garden's relation to the home

You have the Bagua in one hand and a magazine photo of the garden of your dreams in the other. Now what? Don't just stand there! Make that dream come true. Trust us, you can do it. In this chapter, we help you design the garden of your dreams — a Feng Shui garden of your dreams, that is.

By making good choices before the first seed is planted, you can create a delightful Feng Shui garden that welcomes you and your guests with warmth and abundance, or at least without unpleasant squishing sounds under your shoes (dog poop, though natural, is very un-Feng Shui). We think you may find it much easier to Feng Shui by design than to uproot hedges that have been in existence longer than you have, so if you're faced with a lot full of sod and mud and not much else — great! We can show you how to turn that barren landscape into a garden showcase.

In this chapter, we help you figure out what functions you want your garden to perform. (No, we don't mean doing the laundry or waiting on tables. We wish. We mean providing a space for entertaining and things like that.) We also show you why the right physical location is crucial to your garden's success. And we give you tips and fixes for handling location problems if you can't sell your house and get a new one with a better garden location.

If the first seed in your garden was planted long before you grew your first tooth (or even more recently than that), turn to Chapter 6, which gives you plenty of ideas for making an existing, established garden more Feng Shui friendly.

Figuring Out Your Garden's Purpose

Before you dig the first flowerbed, you need to know what you want to do with your garden, or at least what you want to do *in* your garden.

Landscape architect and contributor to this book Herb Schaal encourages gardeners to create a contemplative garden. "It's emotionally healthy and therapeutic," he says. Such a place consists of a quiet, serene area where you can "lose yourself in the spirit of nature." This contemplative place doesn't have to take up the whole garden — a little spot tucked away around a corner can be a relaxing getaway from the day's cares. See the section, "Making a garden for relaxation," later in this chapter for more information.

Of course, a garden can — and probably will — have more than one purpose. But deciding ahead of time what you want to do in your garden keeps you (or more likely your kids) from playing volleyball in the vegetable garden.

Good Feng Shui comes from good design, so don't skimp on this essential element of garden planning!

Creating a garden for play

If you have children, dogs, or a weekend warrior in your family, then you know that you need to set aside part of your yard for play, preferably a flat part (horseshoes is a little hard to play if one team is playing on the top of a hill).

A play area for children should include hands-on activities — a place where they can change things around at their own whims, where they can dig, get messy, and be creative.

Plan to include swing sets and sandboxes for younger children, and set aside space for your older children to play catch, chase the cat, and set up pup tents.

Ask the kids what they want included in the garden. You may find that they're more interested in bird-watching than in building forts. You can accommodate their interests more easily if you know what their interests are! Do plan on making the final determination of how your garden grows yourself, however.

Living energy — in this case, kids — raises the chi in a garden, so having a place they can play in the yard is good for everyone.

Just keep in mind that kids generate lots of yang energy, so if they're playing (shouting shrilly, throwing footballs, daring each other to jump over the retaining wall) right next to your quiet, yin energy contemplative spot, you might end up with conflicting energy patterns — and frustration for everyone.

Separate the play and the contemplative spots in your garden. You don't want to end up spiking the ball into the lily pond (although we realize that has its own attraction). You can physically separate two different functions by placing them at different ends of the yard, or by adding barriers such as hedges and retaining walls. If your yard is too small for separate areas, be creative and think versatility. Choose a folding chaise lounge that can be moved out of the way for pick-up basketball and pots that can be scooted around instead of flowerbeds.

Making a garden for relaxation

You can create an entire garden based on the theme of relaxation (see Chapter 16). Or you can just set aside a quiet corner, furnish it with a bench under a shady tree, and perhaps add a water fountain bubbling nearby (a nice cooler for liquid refreshment wouldn't hurt, either). A relaxing garden nook doesn't have to be complicated — in fact, the simpler the better. Try to

- Choose a quiet spot away from house and road noise
- Keep your relaxation/contemplation spot out of direct sunlight because at certain times of the year, the sun beating down relentlessly on you can make the spot a tad uncomfortable
- Add a bird feeder, pond, or other attraction if you like contemplating nature while relaxing (see Chapter 11 for more on attracting wildlife)
- Design a gazebo or arbor for your contemplative spot to ensure some privacy and peace while offering a bit of comfort
- Plant your favorite bushes and flowers to delight your senses while you're relaxing

See Figure 5-1 for a quiet garden spot.

Photo courtesy of author

Figure 5-1: This wood swing is placed in a quiet corner of the garden.

Entertaining others in your garden

Your garden can be an extension of your living room if you plan it that way. You can entertain guests outdoors for most of the year, unless you live in, say, Minnesota, in which case you can entertain guests outdoors for two weekends in July.

Turning the guests out of doors reduces the number of spills on the carpet and furniture, which may be important for those of you who are fastidious types. Having an outdoor option is especially important if the living area in your home is small.

Of course, if you're a confirmed curmudgeon, you can skip this section and go directly to "Gardening for fun and profit" (and if you're a confirmed curmudgeon, you already did that).

To make your garden welcoming to guests, consider the following ideas:

- A screened-in porch offers guests some protection from the elements (and the mosquitoes) while also allowing them a feeling of being out in nature.
- A deck or patio where guests can gather, mingle, chat, eat, and drink helps ensure a successful party or get-together. Placing a keg on said deck or patio is also favorable.
- Place the entertainment area of your garden near an entrance to your home so that people can move back and forth between the two — truly making the garden an extension of your home. Make certain the pathways to and from the entrance and near the entrance are unobstructed.
- Consider your guests' comfort. Have chairs, tables, and lighting available to them.
- Adding an outdoor stereo, kitchen area (including grill), heaters, fans, and other comforts can help create a very entertaining garden.

See Figure 5-2 for a garden that entertains.

© 2004 EDAW — photography by Dixi Carrillo

Figure 5-2: A garden meant for entertaining.

Gardening for fun and profit

The kitchen garden (see Chapter 18) and the aromatherapy-herbal garden (see Chapter 13) are examples of gardening for more than visual appeal. You can eat the produce you grow, saving money and making meals more appetizing. (A store-bought tomato can never compare to one freshly picked from the vine outside your kitchen door.)

Gardeners with large yards often produce enough fruits and veggies to sell them at local farmers' markets or at roadside stands. If you can't envision yourself hawking jars of hot peppers to tourists, you can at least give the peppers away to friends and family.

Growing edible plants makes a great family pastime, but don't fool yourself that the kids are going to do very much of the work. They enjoy picking out the seeds and helping to plant them, but plan to do much of the watering and weeding yourself.

Combining more than one function

Different parts of the yard or garden can be set aside for different activities. Design the various parts of the garden so the different functions work together. For example, you may want to keep the vegetable garden away from the play area (to avoid footballs bouncing in the tomatoes), but the play area and the entertaining area just might complement each other.

In a small yard, the space used for entertaining can also double as a space for playing active sports. That is, a relatively flat, clear area can do both jobs. When you're entertaining, you can quickly set up some tables and chairs in this area; when you're ready to play, you can convert it by moving the tables and chairs out of the way or storing them in a shed or garage. Be creative about how to get the most from your garden!

Finding the Best Location

Feng Shui says location, location, location! To reap the benefits of Feng Shui, you need to place your garden in the most auspicious location.

- Choose a site that's protected from the worst weather, especially winds. In other words, avoid the mountaintop and settle for part way down the slope.
- Keep in mind that you want chi to move smoothly throughout your garden, so if something about the location would prevent that, rethink the location. See Chapter 4 for more information on chi.
- An ideal location for your garden is in an area protected from the elements — a valley, a grove, or other naturally protected environment.

Identifying inappropriate locations

Certain locations pose problems for your garden. Not all of these location problems can be corrected, so choose a good location to start with. Even when Feng Shui location fixes can be put into action (see Chapter 12), they're often limited in how much good they can do.

Classical Feng Shui instructor and contributor to this book P.K. Odle says that the following locations should be avoided:

- **Over or near public sewage lines, landfills, and dumpsites:** Such places can create negative energy — and who wants a garden situated near waste and refuse?
- **Over or near a cemetery or burial ground or near a funeral parlor:** Although you can sometimes block the view, the negative energies still affect your environment.
- **Near a hospital or police station:** Negative vibes, man, negative vibes.
- **The top of a hill, especially if exposed:** The chi swiftly moves around this location. Adding barriers to stop the chi from hitting you directly helps (for example, plant trees and shrubs and put up a solid fence).
- **Near a large rushing river or large body of water:** Planting thick shrubs or trees between the water and the garden and/or building can help prevent chi from being carried away from your garden.
- **At the end of a dead-end street:** The flow of chi is blocked.

- **At the top of a T- or an I- intersection:** Roads, like rivers, carry chi toward and away from your environment. Having your garden at the top of an intersection can create a negative arrow of rushing chi aimed at your garden. Creating a barrier such as a hedge can help.
- **At the outer edge of a curving road or near an overpass:** Chi is pulled away from your garden. Plus, you're hit by the chi coming off the outside of the curve. Planting a hedge helps contain the chi while blocking the direct hit of chi.

How much enjoyment you get out of your garden may depend on where you locate it. The poor locations previously described are considered inappropriate in Feng Shui because of the impact they have on your environment's energy and the flow of chi.

Keep in mind that inappropriate locations can be harmful for other reasons, too. For example, one gardening couple lives a few blocks from a heavily traveled highway. Although they have a privacy fence to act as a barrier, the noise from the highway makes it difficult for them to enjoy their backyard garden in peace.

Judging the impact of the surrounding environment

Objects in the environment surrounding the garden also affect the garden itself. P.K. Odle points out that certain objects in the surrounding environment can create negative energy.

Some of these problems can be corrected, but others cannot, so again, choose a different place for your garden, if possible:

- **Large high-tension power lines:** These babies burn off energy in your environment. The closer the lines are, the more energy they burn off. This problem cannot be corrected.
- **Utility poles with transformers:** These burn off energy. An Earth element (concrete statue or bench, stone or brick wall) can be positioned between the pole and the garden — because Earth can extinguish Fire — and the utility pole with a transformer is a Fire element. In Figure 5-3, a concrete statue and stone wall, both objects of the Earth element, are placed between the pole and the garden to prevent some energy burn off.

Photo courtesy of author

Figure 5-3: The Earth element objects here prevent some energy burn off.

- **Traffic signal boxes:** These burn off energy. Because they're a Fire element, an Earth element can work to counteract the effect.
- **Sharp corners aimed at the entrance to the garden:** These create a direct hit of chi, which always has a negative effect when pointed at an entrance. Block the negative chi with a tree or other barrier.
- **Tall buildings:** A garden overshadowed by tall buildings can be uncomfortable — the tall buildings can seem oppressive. You cannot correct this problem.

Getting the most auspicious shape

The most favorable shape for a garden is a regular square or rectangle. The Bagua can be placed over the garden plan and all the life sectors are accounted for (see Chapters 3 and 6 for more information about the Bagua and the Life Sectors). Oddly shaped gardens aren't good Feng Shui because sectors of the Bagua tend to be missing or incomplete. Circular gardens also aren't the best choice because the chi moves too swiftly through them.

According to P.K. Odle, if your garden area is oddly shaped, you can use plants or solid fences to make your garden area square or rectangular.

Designing Your Garden around Your Home

To design a welcoming, inviting Feng Shui garden, you need to consider function and location (see the sections above, "Figuring Out Your Garden's Purpose" and "Finding the Best Location") as well as the relation of the house to the garden. The house and the garden should really be considered one unit, rather than separate environments.

Front, back, and side yards: The garden in relation to the home

Most people have several yards or gardens extending from their homes. A person standing in the street can see your front yard as well as side yards on both the left and right sides of the house. You probably also have a backyard that may be enclosed and separate from the more public front and side yards.

When planning to Feng Shui your garden, you need to take all of these possible gardens into consideration — and also think about how they relate to the home.

- The home should be the center of the garden.
- You should be able to easily enter and exit the garden from your home.
- The view from your windows should be attractive and appealing. (In other words, move the compost pile to the far side of the yard.)

Creating and analyzing a site plan

Before investing time, energy, and money in a garden, create a site plan to help you check for potential Feng Shui problems. Making a site plan before you actually buy your home is your best bet (you can identify and turn down inappropriate locations), but a plan is also helpful after you've already chosen your home's location (you can identify and possibly cure any major location problems).

The significance of each yard

As Feng Shui consultant and contributor to this book Jayme Barrett points out, each yard surrounding a typical home has a different impact:

- **The backyard equals the future.** In other words, the backyard symbolizes what might happen in your own future. So if the plants grow abundantly, you're helping to ensure an abundant future for yourself. If the area is neglected and sad, uh-oh — you're writing your own destiny!
- **The front yard makes a strong first impression on guests.** Because guests see it as they approach your home, you want them to feel a sense of welcome. Keeping the front yard clean and neat shows visitors that you value and respect your home.
- **The left side yard is auspicious for a healthy family.** According to the Bagua, this part of the yard is related to the Family life sector. To ensure good relationships with your family members, keep it looking sharp!
- **The right side yard promotes creativity.** According to the Bagua, this part of the yard is related to the Children sector (also known as the Creativity sector). In order to stay creative and unblocked, you want this side yard to be clutter free and bountiful.

Although, in some cases, no cure exists for a Feng Shui problem, you can at least recognize the problem and work around it as much as possible. For example, if high-tension power wires overhang a corner of your back yard, you may want to move the entertainment function to a space in your yard away from the lines. The problem still exists, but at least it doesn't represent as much of a challenge during your family get-togethers. Enough Fire energy is probably generated by confrontations between Grandma and Cousin Joe.

Making the site plan

To create a site plan, follow these steps:

1. **Sketch a drawing of your home and landscape, showing just the basics — the road in front of your house, the alley behind it, the front, back, and side yards, and the position of your house.**
2. **Go outside and take a walk around the house. Notice — and sketch down — potential problems you see, such as overhead lines, utility poles, or a towering building across the street.**

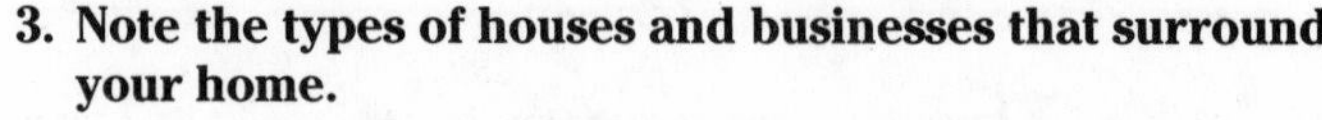

3. **Note the types of houses and businesses that surround your home.**

   In a typical suburban neighborhood, most of the houses are similar to yours, which is fine; in a more eclectic neighborhood, you might be across the street from the local power plant, which can cause some Feng Shui concerns.

4. **After noting this information on your site plan, remember the functions your garden may need to perform. List the most important functions (for example, a play area for children and a contemplative spot for you) and sketch various locations for these areas.**

Analyzing the site plan

After you finish the sketch, check it over with the help of the information in this chapter. Make solving any problems you identify a priority. If, for example, you discover that you're on the curve of a road (see "Identifying Inappropriate Locations" above), you may decide to cure it by adding a hedge. You can fix that problem before you plant the kitchen garden.

The site plan simply shows you the main functions of your garden and where these functions would best be located. The plan also shows you any major Feng Shui challenges you need to correct. In Chapter 6, we show you how to turn that site plan into a garden plan you can use every step of the way.

Chapter 6

Putting Feng Shui to Work in Your Garden

In This Chapter

- Making a site plan for your new garden
- Using the Bagua to raise chi
- Keeping the Five Elements balanced

Before you start digging, you need to plan how you're going to use the Five Elements and the Bagua to ensure the smooth flow of chi (life energy) throughout your environment. (See Chapter 3 for more information on the Five Elements, the Bagua, and chi.) Chi that flows smoothly throughout your garden creates a pleasant and inviting place to visit. (You may even want to live there.) Even if you've already planted your garden, we can help. This chapter gives you insight into how to work with an existing garden to make it more Feng Shui.

In this chapter, we show you how to use the Five Elements and the life sectors of the Bagua to create abundance in your garden — and in your life! The Five Elements and the Bagua are important principles of Feng Shui and using them together in your garden helps raise the chi. Chi brings abundance into your garden and into your life.

Chi not only makes you feel good, but, according to Feng Shui, it even helps your plants grow. A thriving garden makes you feel good. A thriving Feng Shui garden actually enhances your life by symbolically (and literally) improving areas of your life that you feel are lacking.

Creating a New Plan for Your Old Garden

To make your old garden over into a Feng Shui garden, you first need to create a site plan. In Chapter 5, we talk about creating a site plan that shows the functions of your current garden and any potential Feng Shui location problems that it may have. Use your site plan as a starting point for planning your Feng Shui garden. (If you didn't create the site plan before, do so now.)

Make two copies of the site plan, labeling one "Current Garden Plan" and one "Feng Shui Garden Plan." As you may imagine, these two plans will be slightly different. The Current Garden Plan reflects what you have; the Feng Shui Garden Plan reflects what you want to have.

Take your current plan and sketch in any landscaping that your garden currently has. Indicate paths, walkways, driveways, decks, patios, garden structures, outdoor furniture, lighting fixtures, plants, trees, shrubs, and windows and entrances to your house.

To help you create your current site plan, take photographs of your garden from various angles. You can mark these photos with ideas for your garden. Keep the site plan and the photographs in a folder so you can easily refer to them as you plan your new garden.

Evaluating your current site plan

When evaluating your current site plan, consider any Feng Shui location problems you have to fix. For instance, you may need to add a barrier, such as a hedge, to keep the chi from leaving your garden too quickly. (Chapter 5 discusses potential location problems in detail.) See Figure 6-1 for an example.

After identifying any potential location problems, ask yourself whether your current garden adequately performs its functions. You may need to make some changes. For example, if the kitchen garden is too close to the play area, perhaps you can move the kitchen garden next to the contemplation area. Or maybe you can move one function to the side yard or the front yard.

Photo courtesy of author

Figure 6-1: This hedge prevents chi from leaving the garden too quickly.

Consider anything else you want or need to change for practical reasons. For example:

- Cut down an old tree.
- Take out some dying shrubs.
- Scout your property for eyesores.
- Watch out for cluttered plants that don't grow well where they're currently located and any other landscaping problems.

You'll take care of these problems when you start implementing your Feng Shui garden plan (see the next section).

Making a Feng Shui garden plan

Mark any changes you want to make in your current garden on your Feng Shui garden plan. For example, mark where you intend to incorporate more landscaping or a fountain into your garden or where you want to create an area for contemplation.

Later in this chapter, we discuss how to raise the chi in different life sectors of the Bagua. You may want to add some cures to raise the chi; you can mark these cures on your Feng Shui Garden Plan. Also consider making changes to your entrances and walkways in order to allow chi to move more freely throughout your garden (see Chapter 4). Sketch in any necessary changes to your Feng Shui garden plan.

Having two plans — one that shows your current garden and one that shows your dream garden — helps you make comparisons between the two. By retaining a current plan, you can reconsider your dream plan at any time. For example, if costs or the time investment needed for your dream garden get too high, you can reconsider without having to start from scratch.

You can also show the plans to the individuals you consult (for example, a landscape architect, the salesperson at the local nursery) so they can see what you have and what you're trying to do.

You also want to keep in mind how you can raise the chi in the life sectors of the Bagua and how to keep the Five Elements balanced in your garden (see the following sections and Chapter 3 for more on Bagua and the Five Elements). Make notes on your Feng Shui garden plan so that you can keep track of the ideas that you want to follow up on.

Keep your Feng Shui garden plan available as you choose the plants and structures that you want to place in your garden.

Using the Bagua to Enhance Chi

The *Bagua,* which symbolizes the eight directions (north, south, east, west, northeast, northwest, southeast, and southwest) and the nine life sectors (see Chapter 3), can be used as a pattern for raising the chi in your garden. In Feng Shui, each of the eight directions is thought to bring a certain kind of energy with it, and that energy has certain characteristics. In your garden, you want to encourage the energy from each of the directions to enter your garden. You can do this by adding cures or fixes to enhance or raise the chi.

Each of the life sectors of the Bagua has a physical location in your garden and corresponds with an aspect of your life. Raising the chi in one life sector in your environment raises the energy in that sector in your life.

Each life sector is associated with one of the Five Elements. The best way to raise the chi in a specific life sector is to add the element related to that sector. For example, the Fame sector is associated with the Fire element. Adding Fire element to the Fame sector enhances the chi in that sector. So if you want to have a little more Fame in your life (a good reputation, for instance), you raise the chi in that sector of the garden.

Suppose you want to do better in your career. You can raise the chi in the Career sector of the garden and *voilà!* The pay raise you were hoping for appears in next month's paycheck. Well, okay, maybe it won't happen quite like that, but by setting your goals and naming your intentions, you can create good energy that will perk up all parts of your life.

Of course, you could spend all your time raising the chi in the Wealth sector at the expense of the other life sectors. But that would be bad for you! Just like you need to have balance among all aspects of your life, so also do you need to have balance in all the life sectors in your garden. So if you could use a little Wealth, by all means raise the chi in your Wealth sector. But don't forget the Family sector while you're at it!

To orient the Bagua, place the Career sector facing the entrance to the garden. Use the main entrance to the garden if you have more than one entrance. See Chapter 3 for more information.

Fame sector

The Fame sector symbolizes enthusiasm and completion. This sector is associated with the Fire element (see Chapter 3 for more on the Five Elements). To enhance your reputation, raise the chi in the Fame sector of your garden. A good function for this sector would be entertainment — this isn't a spot for quiet contemplation!

If you place the Bagua over your existing garden and you discover that your quiet nook is directly in the middle of the Fame sector, you may want to make some changes. Otherwise, you could find that not much is happening in the Fame sector of your life. Or you may find that people constantly interrupt you as you try to relax in the garden because you've placed a contemplative spot in an area of the garden not meant for it (according to Feng Shui, anyway.)

You can raise the chi in the Fame sector of your garden by planting red flowers or adding red or flame-shaped structures or objects here. Lighting, which represents Fire, also helps increase the chi in this sector. A grill or barbecue, which also symbolize the Fire element, would be a good addition to the Fame sector.

Wood feeds Fire, so adding Wood element enhances the chi in this sector. See Chapter 3 for details on how the elements work together.

Water extinguishes Fire, so use Water element with care in this sector.

Relationships sector

The Relationships Sector is also called the Marriage Sector. It symbolizes close and intimate relationships, so if your marriage needs a little spark, raising the chi in this sector will help. Making this a quiet little spot for the two of you to share a glass of wine before dinner will do wonders for your relationship.

You can raise the chi by planting masses of pink and white flowers in this area of your garden because the color pink is associated with this sector. The Relationships sector is also associated with the Earth element, so adding Earth element helps raise the chi, too. Another way you can enhance the chi in this sector is to add square-shaped objects, such as square planters or square tiles. See Figure 6-2 for an example.

Photo courtesy of author

Figure 6-2: This relaxing spot is made just for two.

Fire makes Earth, so adding Fire element enhances the chi in the Relationships sector.

Wood consumes Earth, so be careful when using the Wood element here — especially woody plants, natural wood objects, and wooden structures. Because you're likely to have the Wood element in a garden (plants symbolize Wood), just keep balance in mind. In Figure 6-2, for example, the Wood plants and chairs are balanced by the stones (Earth element) surrounding the pond.

Children sector

The Children Sector is also called the Creativity Sector. If you want to pump up your creativity, improve your relationship with your kids, or someday have children, enhancing the chi in this sector will increase the odds.

This sector is the perfect spot for group activities, such as volleyball, or for a play area for children. You can also make it a quiet spot for sketching and painting if you don't have kids and don't like volleyball. See Figure 6-3 for an example.

© 2004 EDAW — photography by Dixi Carrillo

Figure 6-3: This play structure can entertain kids all day long.

The Children sector is associated with the Metal element. White and pastel colors, which are associated with the Metal element, raise the chi in this area: Think white outdoor furniture and play equipment. Anything made of metal will also raise the chi, including objects such as brass planters or metal sculptures.

Earth creates Metal, so adding the Earth element to this sector enhances the chi. Objects associated with Earth include stone and ceramic. Also, the color yellow is associated with Earth.

Fire melts Metal, so be careful of using Fire element, such as grills, barbecue pits, candles, and red objects. If kids play in this area, the warning is doubly important.

Helpful People sector

The Helpful People sector is also called the Travel sector. This sector is a good spot for statuary and symbolic guardians of your property. (We're hoping to someday inherit the lions that flank the entrance to the New York Public Library . . . until then, we have to be satisfied with our garden gnomes.)

To increase the chi in this sector — and to attract helpful people to your life — use the color gray, circular shapes, and the Metal element. A metal bench encircling a tree, for example, can enhance the chi in this sector. Also, adding artifacts from your travels enhances the chi. Perhaps you picked up an interesting rock from Peru; putting it in this sector will improve the chi.

Earth creates Metal, so adding Earth element to this sector increases the chi. Think of adding objects made of stone, ceramic, and clay.

Fire melts Metal, so be wary of the Fire element in this sector. You may want to avoid the color red, objects related to Fire such as fireplaces, and flame or triangle shaped objects.

Career sector

The Career sector enhances your career prospects. This area can be a quiet spot — a place where you can do a bit of work when you feel like it. The sector is associated with black and dark blue colors and the Water element, so a fountain is the perfect way to raise the chi in this sector. Also think about including dark-colored outdoor furniture in this area of your garden. A black cast iron table, for example, is a good choice. The color black is associated with the Career sector and the Metal element supports the Water element.

Avoid having a play area here if you want your career to flourish (most people's careers are associated with work, not with play). Including a vegetable patch in this sector is a good idea because it symbolizes production and abundance, which (we assume) you want in your career. See Figure 6-4 for an example.

Metal holds Water, so the Metal element enhances the chi in this sector, making the cast iron table we mentioned doubly effective.

Figure 6-4: The water feature and dark-colored throw enhance chi in the Career sector.

Earth blocks Water, so don't add too much Earth element to this sector.

Knowledge sector

The Knowledge sector is associated with gaining a deeper understanding of the universe, especially spiritual matters. This area is the perfect spot for a contemplative garden (see Chapters 16 and 17). Simply adding a stone bench can enhance the chi in this sector.

This sector is associated with the color blue and with the Earth element. A pond, waterfall, or water fountain can enhance the chi in this area, as can an Earth element object, such as a stone sundial or brick pathway.

Fire makes Earth, so adding Fire element to this sector enhances the chi (think the color red, flame-shaped objects, and lighting). Wood consumes Earth, so place less emphasis on the Wood element here (plants, shrubs, wicker, and bamboo).

Family sector

The Family sector is associated with growth and new ideas and with nurturing family relationships. This sector is the perfect spot for family gatherings. You can create a picnic area here or start a family kitchen garden (see Chapter 18 for more on creating a kitchen garden).

The Family sector is associated with the color green and with the Wood element. Because all plants are part of the Wood element, adding a lot of plants to this sector raises the chi. You can also use bamboo and wicker furniture and accessories (more Wood element) in this area to raise the chi. A patch of green lawn or green leaves enhances the chi, too — plants are Wood element and green is the color associated with Wood, so you get a two-fer! See Figure 6-5 for an example.

Water nurtures Wood, so adding the Water element to this sector raises the chi. You can add a fish pond or a waterfall.

© 2004 EDAW — photography by Dixi Carrillo

Figure 6-5: This arrangement invites friends and family to stay a while.

Metal cuts Wood, so avoid putting too much of the Metal element in this sector.

Wealth sector

The Wealth sector is associated with abundance and prosperity of all types (not just financial). This sector is a good place for a pond or waterfall because water flowing toward the house symbolizes abundance flowing toward you.

The Wealth sector is associated with the Wood element and is symbolized by the color purple — so plant purple flowers galore! Because all plants are Wood elements, plant plenty of them in this sector to keep the abundance flowing. You can also add wicker or bamboo furniture to this area of your garden to enhance the Wood element.

Fruit trees, especially orange trees if you can grow them in your climate, are very auspicious here. Oranges symbolize gold and prosperity in Feng Shui.

Water nourishes Wood, so adding water features, such as fountains, streams, or fish ponds, work well in the Wealth sector.

Putting the compost pile in the Wealth sector decays your wealth! Also avoid metal furniture or other metal items in the Wealth sector because Metal element cuts (destroys) Wood element.

T'ai Chi sector

The T'ai Chi sector, which is in the center of the garden, symbolizes your overall health and well-being. The color yellow is associated with this sector, so bring on the daisies and the sunflowers to raise the chi!

The T'ai Chi sector, also called the Health sector, is associated with the Earth element, so adding Earth element to the sector raises the chi (stone, ceramic, tile).

Jayme Barrett, Feng Shui consultant and contributor to this book, suggests adding a labyrinth (maze) in the center of the garden for contemplation and spiritual centering.

The T'ai Chi is balanced when the other eight life sectors are balanced. So get to work on them first!

Balancing the Five Elements Throughout Your Garden

The Five Elements must be balanced in your garden in order to ensure the smooth, free flow of chi throughout the environment. As we mention in Chapter 3, too much of one element upsets the balance and can create negative energy. Negative energy can make you feel anxious and irritable, and even aggressive; it can also make you feel depressed and down.

Each of the Five Elements is associated with a certain area (or areas) of the Bagua (see the previous section, "Using the Bagua to Enhance Chi") and should be used in connection with it. Otherwise, you may inadvertently cancel out a cure you had used to fix a Feng Shui problem (see Chapter 5).

In other words, if you carefully added Fire element to your Fame sector because you wanted to enhance your reputation by raising the chi there, and then you place a nice water fountain in the same sector, you've just used Water element to extinguish Fire element! You haven't enhanced the chi, you've doused it.

The nourishing and controlling cycles of the Five Elements show how each element supports or diminishes the other elements around it. See Chapter 3 for more information.

Water element

The Water element, symbolized by dark colors such as dark blue and black, is present in water features (ponds, fountains, waterfalls, birdbaths, and so on) as well as glass and crystal. Refer to Figure 6-4. Hanging a crystal from a tree branch enhances the Water element in an area where a water feature can't conveniently be placed. A glass-topped table can also symbolize the Water element in your garden (you can take the glass inside during storms).

The Water element is associated with the Career sector of the Bagua. The Water element is associated with irregular, flowing shapes.

Knowing how each of the Five Elements affects each other is important when you're planning your garden (see Chapter 3 for complete details). Remember that

- Water nurtures Wood
- Earth blocks Water

So to increase the Water element in your garden, add Metal element to it; to decrease the Water element, add Earth element.

Wood element

The Wood element, symbolized by greens and blues, is associated with plants, trees, shrubs, and objects such as bamboo, wicker, and natural fabrics (such as cotton). Your garden is likely to have an abundance of Wood element because of all the plants inhabiting it.

The Wood element is associated with the Wealth and Family sectors of the Bagua. The Wood element is connected to rectangular shapes. Remember that

- Water nurtures Wood
- Metal cuts Wood

To increase the Wood element, add Water element to your garden. To reduce the Wood element, add Metal element.

Earth element

The Earth element, which is symbolized by yellows and earth tones, is associated with soil, ceramics, tile, and brick. The Earth element is also associated with stone and terra cotta.

To increase the Earth element in your garden, you can add stone benches and pebble or brick walkways. Stone and terra cotta statuary also increase the Earth element.

The Earth element is associated with the Knowledge and Relationships sectors of the Bagua. The Earth element is connected to square shapes.

Remember that

- Fire makes Earth
- Wood consumes Earth

To increase the Earth element in your garden, incorporate some Fire elements. To decrease the Earth element, add Wood elements. See Figure 6-6 for an example.

Figure 6-6: This stone pathway is a great way to add Earth element to your garden.

Metal element

The Metal element, symbolized by white and pastel colors, is associated with objects made of iron, brass, gold, silver, and other metals. You can increase the Metal element in your garden by adding metal furniture (for example, cast iron tables and chairs) and metal fixtures such as lights.

The Metal element is associated with the Children and Helpful People sectors of the Bagua. The Metal element is connected with circular shapes.

When planning your garden, remember that

- Earth creates Metal
- Fire melts Metal

To increase the Metal element in your garden, add Earth element. To decrease it, include Fire element. See Figure 6-7 for an example.

Photo courtesy of author

Figure 6-7: This bench represents Metal element. Notice the circular back, the shape associated with Metal element.

Fire element

The Fire element, symbolized by the color red, is associated with objects such as lights and candles. You can increase the Fire element in your garden by adding candles, fireplaces, grills, and so on.

The Fire element is associated with the Fame sector. The Fire element is connected with flame or triangular shapes.

Remember that

- Wood feeds Fire
- Water extinguishes Fire

To increase the Fire element, introduce Wood element to your garden. To decrease the Fire element, include Water element.

Chapter 7

Growing the Natural Way

In This Chapter

- Controlling pests and diseases organically
- Saying goodbye to weeds
- Nourishing the soil
- Reducing water consumption
- Using natural materials

According to the principles of Feng Shui, taking the natural approach in your garden by choosing natural materials and native plants is *auspicious* (good for you).

And although growing your garden the natural way makes good sense from a Feng Shui point of view, it also has other benefits. Using natural methods and materials is often more economical than using inorganic chemicals, and it's better for the environment and your own health!

In this chapter, we let you know how to use organic and natural means and methods to keep pesky pests out of your garden (we're sorry, we can't do anything about the in-laws!). We also show you how to fertilize without harsh chemicals, use natural materials, and even conserve water.

Practicing Natural Pest and Disease Control

In Chapter 11, we show you how to use barriers (fences and the like) to keep pesky mammals at bay. But to keep away other pests — for example, the ones with wings — you need to take a different approach.

Careful planning and maintenance in your garden can help keep it pest-free. And if you do end up with a few annoying critters, you'll be able to make short work of them. Always try to make the natural choice when you're thinking about how to get rid of all those webworms and aphids instead of automatically breaking out the big guns (inorganic chemicals that end up in the groundwater).

Designing healthy gardens

Start by planning wisely. If you choose *native plants* (plants that grow naturally in your climate and terrain), you're already ahead of the game. These plants know how to survive where you live, and they can accommodate stresses that non-native plants would croak over.

Specifically, choose plants proven to be disease- and insect-resistant for your area. In some places, drought-resistant (or at least drought-tolerant) plants make good choices. (Think Arizona in the middle of summer.) Ask for recommendations at your local nursery or *extension agency* (a joint federal and state service that provides information about agriculture and home economics to interested individuals; most counties have an extension agency).

After you've decided what'll work best for your area, buy only the healthiest plants, seeds, and bulbs. If you see brown or bare spots, rotten roots, or insect infestations, just say no. Be very picky when it comes to what you put in your garden, and you'll save yourself a lot of headaches down the road.

Some plants attract pests that are already in the environment, so that even if you buy the plant pest-free, it'll soon be full of bagworms, spider mites, and other icky bugs. Contact your extension agency to find out which plants are most susceptible to the pests in your local environment.

After you get some healthy plants, keep them healthy. Healthy plants combat disease and insects much better than stressed plants. The following steps will help you:

- Keep the soil in good condition. (See the section "Building the Soil" later in this chapter for more information.)
- Fertilize plants — but with restraint. (See the section, "Building the Soil" later in this chapter for more information.)
- Don't overcrowd plants.
- Allow plenty of air circulation.
- Make sure plants have plenty of root room.

Controlling pests

What if, despite carefully choosing the most pest-free plants for your garden, you still end up with a pest problem? Well, read on and find out what to do.

Assessing the situation

First, make sure that you actually do have a pest problem. Sometimes the signs of disease may, at first glance, resemble insect damage. Disease, not surprisingly, requires a different cure than pests. (See the section, "Combating disease" later in this chapter for further information.)

Next, assess the need for intervention. Sometimes, if you notice bugs but no damage to your plants, you don't have to do anything. The natural predators in your garden will take care of the pests for you.

A bug taking a few chomps out of a leaf probably does not require blasting your entire landscape with chemical pesticides.

Your local nursery or extension agency can help you distinguish between pest damage and disease damage, and can also help you identify which bugs are bugging your plants.

Taking action

If you must swing into action, start with the least damaging and least toxic approach first. For example, when a light infestation of Japanese beetles attacked one gardener's plants, she just collected them in a bottle of soapy water and drowned them. End of problem. Only if an approach like this one fails should you go to the next level.

The list below offers some approaches you can take, going from least invasive to more invasive.

- **Timing:** Plant according to pest life cycles. If your plant flowers before or after its most common pests have matured, you'll have fewer problems.
- **Beneficial bugs:** Keep beneficial bugs around. See Chapter 11 for more information.
- **Microorganisms:** Use mini-bugs to keep pests at bay. In other words, use a specific insect disease to kill a specific type of insect. You can buy Milky Disease spores to kill Japanese beetles without harming beneficial bugs or your plants. Nematodes are parasites you can mix with water and spray on your lawn. They'll eat up grubs without damaging plants.

- **Barriers:** Place nets (or "floating row covers") over plants to keep pests away from your tasty vegetables. See Chapter 11 for information on fences and other barriers.
- **Bands:** Wrap copper bands around plant stems to keep slugs away. Collars (plastic or felt) can prevent root flies from attacking plants. Tree bands secured around the trunks of your trees keep crawling pests away.
- **Traps:** Use a biological or chemical bait to attract pests. Some traps, like bug zappers, kill good insects along with the bad. Uh-oh.
- **Hand removal:** Pick the bugs off by hand. This approach is most useful for small infestations of large bugs. You can also use a handheld vacuum for this purpose. (They don't show this use on the TV commercials, but it works!)
- **Water Sprays:** Spray plants with water to knock off critters like aphids.
- **Organic Sprays:** Apply organic sprays only if other approaches fail. Even though these are better for your garden than inorganic chemicals, they can still be toxic, so use with care. Insecticidal soap can destroy aphids without too much damage to beneficial insects. Horticultural oils can also be used to control beetles and caterpillars, but they can damage plants, so proceed with caution. Check with your local nursery for the best organic sprays for your area.

Combating disease

Your best bet is to start with healthy, disease-resistant plants. (See the section "Designing healthy gardens" earlier in this chapter for more information.)

Dead and dying plants are bad Feng Shui. They depress the energy in your garden. Take steps to keep your plants healthy and get rid of those that aren't.

As Mama always said, an ounce of prevention is worth a pound of cure. So to prevent plant diseases from taking hold and spreading:

- Keep your hands clean. Don't spread a disease from one plant to another.
- Regularly disinfect your tools and other gardening equipment (even your gardening shoes and gloves!).
- Use care to prevent damaging plants when mowing or trimming.
- Prune diseased plants — and disinfect the pruner afterwards.

Whodunnit?

You may automatically assume that a problem you're having with a plant is owing to a bug or a disease. But it might be the environment instead! So before you start hunting down those aphids, consider the following:

- Stunted growth and discolored leaves could signal a nutritional deficiency or pollution.
- Cracked bark on your trees could be the result of too much cold weather.
- Wilting and discolored leaves could be caused by lack of water.
- Scorched-looking leaves may be suffering from wind damage.

- Pull up and discard diseased small plants or badly diseased larger plants.
- Keep your garden clean. Some diseases *overwinter* (go dormant and survive the cold) in litter (fallen leaves, for example). Cleaning the clutter is also good Feng Shui.
- Don't compost any plant material that looks diseased.

Chances are, following these steps will cut down on disease in your garden. But if you have an outbreak that needs more aggressive treatment, use some thought before investing in a sack full of chemical products from the local garden center. Many of these products are unhealthy for you and the environment. Instead, try an organic approach to treating disease:

- Microbial fungicides can prevent disease without blighting the landscape.
- Vegetable oil sprayed on plants can prevent diseases (it acts as a barrier).

See *Gardening For Dummies,* 2nd Edition, by Mike MacCaskey and Bill Marken (Wiley) for complete information on handling diseases and pests in the garden.

Getting Rid of Weeds

If you put your mind to it, you can find even a dandelion attractive. But weeds can be annoying in the garden (and in the lawn). They tend to choke out the plants that you want, and they can provide a handy little habitat for pests and diseases. (Pests and diseases often overwinter in weeds, meaning you'll have to deal with them again next year.)

Weeds require immediate action. If you wait too long, they'll set seed, and then instead of having to pull up one dandelion, you'll have to pull up three thousand dandelions. (Your five-year-old kid may find this amusing, but you won't.)

Because weeds can only grow if soil is available, one way to prevent weed growth is to keep the soil otherwise occupied. You can do this by filling gaps in your garden with ground cover (low-growing plants and grasses that spread quickly) or mulch. Clear the ground of weeds before adding mulch. The best mulch to use is one that's local to your area. Mulch doesn't have to be wood chips; it can be pine needles or bark. Always use organic matter to mulch.

The gentlest way to get rid of weeds is to pull 'em out (gentle on your garden, that is, not on the weeds):

- Use a hoe to get rid of weeds (when possible).
- Fork up big weeds with deep roots.
- Pull up by hand if the hoe or fork could damage surrounding plants (if you damage a plant with your hoe, you may end up with a diseased plant).
- Don't forget to pull up the root so that you don't have to take out the very same weed next week.

Chemical herbicides can damage the growth of the plants you want to keep. They're also not-so-good Feng Shui, because Feng Shui focuses on the natural. Chemical sprays are not nice to Mother Nature and so should be avoided for harmonious Feng Shui. Try to avoid dumping herbicides on your garden. If you must use a weed spray, choose an organic formulation. Some chemical herbicides can be wiped directly on the leaves of the weed; this prevents the herbicide from killing the plants you don't want to kill.

Building the Soil

Starting your garden with good, nutrient-rich soil will help keep your plants sound and healthy. Herb Schaal, landscape architect and contributor to this book, says, "If you have $100 to spend on your garden, spend $90 on the soil. You'll never regret it." Amending soil is hard to do after all the plants are set, so make this a priority before you start planting your zinnias.

You can build the soil by having it analyzed and then amending it with necessary nutrients, or you can bring in a good soil mix. (Herb favors this approach and feels it's well worth the money.)

Healthy soil has all sorts of organisms, minerals, and chemicals that your plants need to thrive. Microbes and earthworms are also present in sound soil. They help decompose decaying plant matter and convert it into nutrients.

When you use chemical pesticides and fertilizers, you can disrupt the balance of nutrients in the soil. Pretty soon, your soil will be chemically dependent. It won't be able to produce a tomato without the intervention of a chemical fertilizer, and pretty soon you'll need to check your yard into rehab. So instead of dumping pesticides and herbicides on your lawn and garden, focus on keeping good quality soil filled with healthy plants — and then you won't need the chemicals.

Composting for success

Make your own compost to help keep your soil nourished without using chemical fertilizers. Composting is also an efficient way of getting rid of yard waste — your grass clippings return to nature instead of getting trucked off to the landfill.

You can compost by dumping plant matter in a loose heap, but that's not very Feng Shui. A loose heap is unattractive, and in Feng Shui, you want to go with clutter-free and attractive. A compost bin is a better choice. You can create your own bin by nailing together some boards to make a box or you can purchase one from a local garden supply store or a mail order organic gardening catalog. A typical compost bin is about 3 feet square.

Compost needs to heat up to decay, so you need to keep the bin partially full at all times to allow this to happen. Keeping that in mind, follow these steps to get great compost:

1. **Put garden waste into the bin. Mix it up nicely so no layer of any one material gets too thick.**
2. **Cover the bin to keep the heat in, the water out, and the smell down. A tarp works fine.**
3. **After a month or so, turn the contents of the bin to let air in and move the outside waste in where it can have a chance to rot (mmm, yum!).**

What to compost?

Your compost pile (bin, heap, box) can be fed with almost any plant matter. Try the following:

- Vegetable peelings
- Discarded plant matter, like apples cores and grape stems
- Weeds
- Grass clippings
- Fallen leaves
- Prunings (as long as they're shredded)

But don't use the following:

- Diseased plant matter
- Cooked food
- Animal products
- Dog and cat manure

The compost will be ready to use after about 2 months during the summer. It will need closer to six months in winter. Keep the compost covered until needed.

Fertilizing your garden frugally

Every gardener itches to get those green things growing in a hurry, which is why you may be tempted to dump a chemical fertilizer on your lawn or garden early in the spring. But before you do, keep in mind that fertilizing your garden can actually damage it.

An overfertilized garden attracts pests (love those lush leaves!) An overfertilized lawn must be mowed more often. Overfertilizing can also destroy beneficial soil organisms. So restrict fertilizing to exactly what you need for your lawn and garden.

On the other hand, if you let the soil get exhausted, your plants won't grow, which is why some fertilizing is sometimes necessary.

Soil contains three primary nutrients:

- Nitrogen (N): For leafy growth
- Phosphorus (P): For healthy roots and ripe fruit
- Potassium (K): For flowering and fruit production

If these nutrients are present in your soil in good quantity, you don't need to fertilize. (Test your soil to find out.) If they're not, you do need to fertilize. Simple, huh? Depending on where you live and the types of plants you're planting, you may only need to fertilize once a year. When you do fertilize:

- **Test the soil first.** Then you can feed it exactly what it needs. You can purchase a test kit from your local extension agency. Less accurate kits can be purchased at garden centers.
- **Pick slow-release fertilizers, such as compost.** You can spread a fine layer on the lawn before a rain and let it soak in. Use it in your garden by working it into the soil or using it like mulch.
- **If you need to add more nutrients to your soil than you can get from compost, choose an organic fertilizer, according to the needs of your soil.** The following are common organic fertilizers that won't harm the environment but will make your plants happy:
    - Bone meal (high in phosphorus)
    - Fish meal
    - Blood meal
    - Hoof and horn (high in nitrogen)
    - Seaweed meal (high in nitrogen)

Don't fertilize lawns during hot, dry spells. Let your grass go dormant instead of watering it and fertilizing it. Doing so makes economical and environmental sense!

Conserving Water

Planning your garden so that it requires a minimal amount of water is environmentally and economically the smart thing to do. And anything that keeps Mother Earth happy is good Feng Shui.

Herb Schaal says that all gardeners should be water conscious, especially in arid or semi-arid climates.

Getting rid of the lawn

No doubt about it, that emerald green blanket of grass is thirsty, thirsty, thirsty. Before rolling the sod out, ask yourself if you really need a traditional suburban lawn.

"Take your cue from the environment around you," Herb says. "In Arizona, the native landscape is sparse and rocky. In Kansas, there's always ground cover." In other words, in Kansas it's smart to have ground cover (not necessarily grass) to keep the moisture in, and in Arizona, it's smart to plant sparingly with native plants, to keep water consumption to a minimum.

Herb Schaal also suggests taking a cue from your neighbors. "Your front yard should be a good citizen with the other yards on the block." So think twice before ripping out the lawn and planting boulders if none of the neighbors are doing the same.

Even so, you can keep your front lawn small. Add plant beds, paths, patios, and decks to your landscape instead of grass. Your yard will still fit in with the neighbors' yards and you'll use less water on it.

You have more flexibility with your backyard. It doesn't have to fit into the neighborhood as much, particularly if you have a fence. So go ahead and do what you will, as long as you follow the principles of Feng Shui.

If you don't want to get rid of your lawn, take a look at these tips for reducing water consumption:

- **Mow less often.** Mowing results in water loss.
- **Keep mower blades higher.** Taller grass tolerates heat better and requires less water.
- **Reduce traffic on the lawn.** Less stressed grass requires less water.
- **Leave grass clippings.** They return moisture to the ground.
- **Let grass go dormant in summer.** Don't worry; your grass isn't dead, and it'll come back.
- **Water deeply but infrequently.** This helps grass develop deep roots to tolerate drought conditions better.
- **Water early in the day or in the evening.** This helps prevent the water from evaporating before the grass can benefit from it.

Water-wise gardening

Plan your garden so that it conserves water. Remember that paths, decks, patios, and the like don't require watering. If you can incorporate them into your garden, you can reduce the amount of watering you need to do.

Other tips for water-wise gardening:

- Add mulch around plants, trees, and shrubs to prevent water evaporation.
- Choose plants that don't require pruning. Pruning stresses plants and causes water loss. If you're pruning plants and shrubs because they're too close together, transplant a few of them.
- Water the soil. Don't spray the leaves (unless you're trying to get rid of a pesky pest, such as the neighbor's cat).
- Established plants don't need regular watering. Water them only when they need it.
- Group plants with similar water needs together. Drought-tolerant plants can go in one place, whereas more fragile plants can go together in another place. This cuts down on your watering duties.

Water conserving gadgets

What would gardening be if you couldn't buy a gadget now and then? The following widgets can help you conserve water, so consider if any of them would be appropriate for your garden:

- **Downspout extensions:** They direct water away from your home's foundation (a good thing) and onto the lawn or garden (which needs the water more than your sidewalk does).
- **Rain barrels:** Instead of a downspout extension, you can place a rain barrel under your downspout to collect water. Choose wood, as natural materials are more Feng Shui than plastic is.
- **Extension handles for hoses:** These connect to your hose and can be used to direct water exactly where you need it.
- **Soaker hoses:** These hoses have little holes in them that can be placed in your garden to deliver water at the base of the plants. Low water pressure keeps the water where it needs to be and reduces runoff.

Building Your Garden with Natural Materials

Using natural materials in your garden creates good energy. Not only is it environmentally sound, but it also creates a more attractive environment. And Feng Shui is all about making things beautiful and welcoming.

Remember the Five Elements as you consider which natural materials to use in your garden. If the object belongs to one of the Five Elements (Earth, Water, Metal, Wood, and Fire), then it's usually fine for the garden. See Chapter 3 for more information on the Five Elements.

For example, although you may not think of metal as being natural, it is. And a cast-iron table (for example), which represents the Metal element, will help balance the Wood element of all those plants in your garden.

But avoid plastics and paints whenever possible. Keep wood plain — no stain needed! Not only is this good Feng Shui, and kind to the environment, but it also makes less work for you!

Make the following choices to create a natural Feng Shui space in your garden:

- Choose waterproof outdoor fabrics instead of plastic. Actually, waterproof fabrics are made from man-made fibers such as acrylic, nylon, and olefin and are heavily coated with urethane, a man-made plastic, but the higher quality ones look and feel nicer (which is always better for Feng Shui purposes) than the discount store thin plastic covered cushions.
- Use wood mulch instead of tarps and landscape fabrics designed to keep weeds out.
- Bamboo and wicker make good alternatives to plastic outdoor furniture.
- Glass table tops and crystal ornaments (perhaps hung from trees) make good natural choices.
- Pave with rock instead of concrete.
- Fence with wood or wrought instead of chain link (which isn't very attractive).

Chapter 8

Preparing a Garden for All Seasons

In This Chapter

- Planning a garden of year-round delights
- Knowing what to plant for the various seasons

Your backyard is your future, according to Feng Shui, so whenever you look out into it, you should see something blooming! Not only is it beautiful, it's auspicious. Also, remember that plants bring living energy into your garden. If they're all dormant, then you have to make extra sure that other sources of energy (squirrels, anyone?) are around.

A Feng Shui garden should be delightful, welcoming, and visually appealing all year round. In some climates, you can pull this off with ease, but in others, you have a challenge ahead of you. In this chapter, we give you some tips for creating a garden that looks gorgeous in each of the four seasons, no matter where you live.

Year-Round Attractions

You want your garden to look attractive throughout the year. Thus, if you select only plants that bloom in the spring, for instance, you have a bedraggled looking environment during summer, fall, and winter. Ugh.

Design your garden so that different plants bloom at different times. Depending on where you live, you can have plants blooming all year long; in climates with actual winters, you can still have plants blooming late into fall and rely on evergreens and hardy shrubs to provide some color in winter.

Take a look at these tips for some pointers on keeping your garden looking its best year-round:

- Keep in mind that your climate, soil conditions, terrain, personal preference, and other factors need to be weighed as you're choosing which plants to include in your garden.
- Choose plants and shrubs that grow and bloom through more than one season to get the most from your garden. (See Table 8-1 for suggestions.) Intersperse them with plants with shorter blooming times. And don't forget to balance the Five Elements (using color, shape, and so on) when choosing your seasonal plant selections.
- Do some gardening chores even in late fall and winter. For example, picking up fallen leaves clears clutter (good Feng Shui) and lightens your gardening load in the spring.
- Arrange structures, terraces, and walls so that even in the depths of winter, your garden looks attractive.

Table 8-1 Plants That Look Attractive through the Seasons

Seasons	*Plants*
Spring through fall	Wormwood, mallow (malva), quince, gardenia, Japanese cherry, Japanese plum
Summer through fall	Monkshood, aconite, Japanese anemone, New England aster, coneflower, wild honeysuckle, cinquefoil
Winter through spring (mild climates)	Violet, windflower, Persian violet, daphne
Year-round	Bougainvillea, in warm weather zones. Sedge, birch tree, box shrub, burning bush, winterberry, crab apple

Springing into Action

Spring is a busy time of year for gardens and gardeners. Now is the time to clear the clutter (for good Feng Shui and healthy plants), remove plants that didn't survive the winter, bring in the annuals, and perform a dozen other gardening tasks.

Thinking about early spring

After a long, dreary winter, the vibrancy of early spring bloomers is a sight for sore eyes. The following plants look gorgeous in early spring and are hardy enough to survive the unpredictable weather:

- Camellia
- Chiondoxa (glory-of-the-snow)
- Crocus
- Daffodil
- Hyacinth
- Iris
- Jonquil
- Sweet cherry tree
- Tulip

Most of these plants come from a bulb, and bulbs are generally planted in fall. So you need to plan ahead of time to create the perfect four-season garden!

Herb Schaal, landscape architect and contributor to this book, also suggests the use of container plants. These plants can be brought outside on sunny spring days and brought inside again when the weather turns nasty. Thus, both your inside and outside environments are brightened with a single flower.

Hanging baskets are also a nice choice for this time of year. If a cold snap comes late, you can bring them indoors to keep them toasty warm.

Mid-spring beauties

Later in spring, the weather is more predictable, and you can choose plants that can't stand a three-dog night but can tolerate a nippy breeze. Some plants that are looking good this time of year include

- Bergenia
- Forsythia
- Magnolia (shrub)
- Narcissus
- Rhododendron

Water features start to come alive this time of year, too. Aquatic plants in your pond start growing, and you may need to divide them. Most aquatic plants are perennial, so if yours aren't blooming, you may need to replace them. You can stock the pond now with fish and plants.

Looking forward to late spring

In the late spring, your kitchen garden starts to wake up (see Chapter 18), so be ready to put out your veggies. Most annuals look good all summer long and can be planted after the threat of frost is over. Also, these plants look gorgeous:

- Azalea
- Broom
- Checkered lily
- Clematis
- Peony
- Phlox
- Wisteria

See Figure 8-1 for a glimpse of a late spring garden.

Photo courtesy of author

Figure 8-1: Late spring lushness.

Savoring Summer's Lazy Days

Summer is a wonderful time for gardening. Plenty of plants can be placed this time of year, including less hardy annuals such as coneflower, cosmos, and dahlias.

Plants (and weeds) grow faster than you can believe, and pests and disease start to poke their way into the garden at this time of year. So you need to be on top of things when summer approaches to keep your garden healthy and beautiful.

Working around the early summer slowdown

A garden may have a few weeks in early summer where it doesn't look as gorgeous as it looked earlier in the spring nor as gorgeous as it will look later in the summer. To prevent such a slowdown, add annuals to your garden mix; they look good all summer long. And turn your attention to attracting butterflies, birds, and, if you want, mammals to your garden to create good living energy for auspicious Feng Shui and to keep your garden looking attractive and welcoming (see Chapter 11 for more information).

Water features become more important now, too. Fountains and waterfalls can run all the time. Ponds should be full of blooming plants and lively fish.

Some plants are showing their stuff at this time. They include the following:

- Buddleia (summer lilac)
- Carnation
- Geranium
- Marigold
- Ornamental onion
- Poppy (perennial)
- Texas bluebonnet

Midsummer relaxation

In midsummer, many of the spring gardening chores are done. The plants are planted; you mainly just need to weed and water. Okay, these aren't the most fun chores, but midsummer does give you a little time to actually get out in your garden and relax.

Create a little spot in the garden with a bench and flowers that bloom this time of year. You can take advantage of the change to sit and relax. Or if you've set aside an area for contemplation, make sure that you've planted it with flowers that bloom at this time of year (see Chapter 5 for more information).

If your summers are very hot, make this spot a pleasant gazebo or locate it near a mature tree that offers ample shade.

If you have an herb garden, start harvesting herbs now. And thin your kitchen garden regularly.

Plants looking pretty good now include

- Alchemilla (lady's mantle)
- Amaranth
- Aster
- Cornflower
- Daisy
- Honeysuckle
- Larkspur
- Lily
- Lobelia
- Morning Glory
- Mullein
- Pansy
- Snapdragon
- Sweet William
- Verbena
- Zinnia

See Figure 8-2 for a midsummer treat.

Maintaining late summer highlights

At this time of year, you can continue to harvest herbs and vegetables. You'll also enjoy these plants, which look good in late summer:

- Blue spire
- Butterfly bush
- Fuchsia
- Mexican sage
- Touch-me-not

Featuring Fall Foliage

Autumn foliage can be breathtaking. Plan to have a least a few trees with leaves that change in fall to add beauty to the garden at this time of year.

Photo courtesy of author

Figure 8-2: Midsummer coneflowers still look gorgeous.

Fall gardening gets a bit busy, because you must plant bulbs for blooming in the spring, clear summer bedding plants, prepare plants for the coming cold, and otherwise take care of business.

Enjoying early autumn experiences

Because early fall weather is often quite beautiful, take advantage of the weather and create spaces in the garden to enjoy the nip in the air.

Although the spring and summer blooms have faded (and should be cleared from the garden), autumn delights still exist. Pick shrubs with bright berries and colored foliage to catch the eye at this season.

See Figure 8-3 for a beautiful fall garden.

Plants looking good right now include

- Autumn crocus
- Black-eyed Susan
- Gladiolus
- Lily of the Field
- Mum
- Pyracantha
- Stonecrop
- Winter daffodil

Photo courtesy of author

Figure 8-3: This garden still looks beautiful in early autumn.

Managing mid-autumn unexpectedness

This time of year the weather is unpredictable. You need to bring in certain bulbs (gladioli) for the winter, and certainly any potted plants should be indoors by now.

Water features need attention now. Before the first frost, fountains and birdbaths should be drained (ice forming in a fountain or birdbath can break it). Ponds require special care: Fish and fragile aquatic plants should be brought indoors.

Think about setting those birdfeeders out soon, because a sharp frost can catch the birds unaware and destroy dinner (see Chapter 11 for more information on birdfeeders).

Here are some plants that get the nod this time of year:

- Apple tree
- Chilean myrtle

- Cyclamen
- Gentian
- Japanese anemone
- Japanese maple
- Witch alder

Looking to late fall marvels

The garden often requires an extra bit of action this time of year to get it ready for winter — mulching the perennials, making certain dead flowers and other clutter is cleared away, and so on.

With some luck and preparation, you can still be harvesting goodies from your kitchen gardens at this time of year (see Chapter 18 for more kitchen gardens). You can still reap lettuce, Chinese cabbage, mustard, broccoli, carrots, and more.

The following plants are looking good this time of year:

- Cotoneaster
- Guernsey lily
- Sweet olive

And don't forget ornamental grasses, which look good even in the snow!

Warming Up for Next Year During Winter

If you plan your garden well, it still exhibits color and energy through the winter months. Plan to use objects as focal points — statuary and other decorative objects attract the eye even more when plants aren't flowering.

See Figure 8-4 for an example of what to do in winter.

Winter is the perfect time for armchair gardening. You can dream up what your garden will look like next spring and order the seeds!

Figure 8-4: Make a statue or decorative object the focus of your winter garden.

Early winter

If the weather holds up, now's the time to mend fences, clear the clutter, and batten down the hatches.

Plants that look attractive now include

- Christmas rose
- Cranberry bush
- Holly
- Jasmine (shrub)
- Witch hazel

Maximizing midwinter quiet

This time of year, most of your gardening tasks take place indoors. Plan and order what you need for next year. Also try to keep the snow and ice off the plants, shrubs, and trees to protect them.

Plants looking good now include

- Snowdrop
- Virburnum
- Winter aconite

Late winter anticipation

This time of year, especially in some climates, the weather turns nicer and it's difficult to keep from planting annuals — but it's much too early. Instead, concentrate on growing seeds indoors. And try out cold frames in the kitchen garden (see Chapter 18).

This time of year, these plants look good:

- Almond tree
- Grape hyacinth
- Lenten rose

Chapter 9

Gardening by Energy Level — Yours!

In This Chapter

- Creating a garden that suits your interests
- Growing a low-maintenance garden
- Pumping up the gardening volume

Making a Feng Shui garden isn't necessarily any more time-consuming or costly than creating some other kind of garden. But any garden can end up costing much more time, energy, and money than you planned for. So in this chapter, we show you how to get the garden you want without having to hire a gardener (or a magician) to get it!

The best gardens don't grow accidentally — and this is even truer for Feng Shui gardens. Without careful thought and planning, you can't create the Feng Shui garden of your dreams. Invest a bit of time before you start digging, and it pays off in the long run.

Getting Started in Stages

Most landscape architects suggest that you start with an overall plan for your garden, called a *site plan.* (See Chapter 5 for information on creating a site plan.) You need an idea of what you want to do with the entire landscape — front yard, backyard, side yards — before you start planting trees. Otherwise you could be halfway through before you realize this ain't gonna work. Do plan to work in stages because applying the principles of Feng Shui to your entire environment takes time and energy.

However, if you're mostly satisfied with what you've got, or if you want to start small to see if this Feng Shui stuff really works, we don't mind. Just remember that something you do now might have to come out next year if you don't start out with the big picture in mind.

After you've got the big picture lined up — you don't necessarily need a lot of details, just the general idea — you can plan your garden activities in stages. For example, stage one could be the front yard (this year), stage two could be the side yards (next year), and stage three could be the backyard (third year).

If you're more of a free spirit and all that planning sounds like a drag, start with the part of your yard that needs the most work, or start with your backyard. Because the backyard represents the future according to Feng Shui, doing some good there results in blessings in your life now and down the road. If you choose to go this way, place the Bagua on the part of the landscape that you're going to be working on. The entrance to the garden should be aligned with the Career sector. See Chapter 3 for more information on placing the Bagua.

Knowing what you want

Creating a garden is a personal thing — like decorating a room. What works for one person may not work for another. Although you're following the principles of Feng Shui as you plan your garden (we're just guessing here), you have a lot of leeway regarding how the garden is designed and what you can put into it. See Chapter 2 for more information.

Knowing what you want sounds a lot simpler than it is. Our friendly landscape architect and contributor, Herb Schaal says, "People are overwhelmed with choice. They walk into a nursery and want one of each." So how do you decide what's right for you?

Simplify, simplify, simplify. Be selective. Herb recommends a three-step process for getting started:

1. **Pick out photographs of gardens you like in magazines and books.**

   Use those pictures to identify what appeals to you.

2. **Take digital images of your environment. Draw on the pictures to show the effect you're trying to create.**

   You may find this method easier to work with than a scaled drawing. If you don't have a digital camera, use a regular camera and draw on the prints or photocopy the prints and draw on the photocopies. It's not quite as effective, but it still works.

3. **Take your photos with you as you visit nurseries.**

   You can see how the plants would fit in the environment. And you can consult with the salespeople, who know which plants are available, which do well in your climate, and whether less costly or hardier plants can be substituted.

Budgeting for garden expenses

In a perfect world, you could pick out whatever you wanted for your garden, and it wouldn't cost you a dime. But you live in the real world, and in the real world, landscaping can be expensive.

- Doing it yourself can save you money, but not if you run the backhoe into the water main. Know when to hire professionals, and calculate those costs into your budget. For example, if you've never dug a posthole in your life, maybe you should hire a contractor to build your privacy fence.
- Although big construction projects (building a deck, putting up a privacy fence) obviously cost money, even smaller projects can get out of hand if you're not careful. A nice tree can cost several hundred dollars. Several nice trees can total $1,000 before you know it. Gulp.
- Get a realistic sense of how much materials cost as you're making your overall plan. If you find out that a wood deck costs $4,000 to build, you may decide to settle for a $500 poured concrete patio.
- Spring and fall are the two most expensive times of year for gardeners. Plants are purchased and planted in both seasons. In the spring, you also need to spend time (and money) replacing structures, plants, and equipment that didn't survive the winter. Plan on added expense during these seasons.
- Replacing plants gets time-consuming and expensive. Choose healthy, native species to get the best bang for your buck.
- Perennials are more expensive than annuals, but some can thrive for years and years, whereas you toss those annuals into the compost bin almost as soon as they're done blooming.
- Beg and borrow plants. If Mom doesn't mind splitting her dahlias with you (and they're healthy), you can save a bundle, plus you get to have a sentimental section in your garden.
- Make a series of priorities and work on your garden according to those priorities: Even if that plum magnolia that has no place in your garden happens to be on sale at the nursery when you go to pick up mulch, don't buy it.

After you've followed this three-step plan, you should have a rough idea of what you want to do. You've identified the structures, trees, shrubs, and plants you want to have. Now you just have to buy 'em and plant 'em.

The chicken or the egg?

As you plan out how you're going to create a beautiful garden, take into consideration that some projects should come before others. For example, suppose you eventually want to put a deck in the backyard. Don't plant a lot of trees and shrubs before the deck goes in because they may have to come up when you do the construction. Likewise, if you're putting up a fence, you want to make sure that you're not going to disturb the $3,000 worth of landscape you just installed. So, first things first:

1. **Construction projects (decks, patios, gazebos)**
2. **Pathways and decorative structures**
3. **Ponds and water features**
4. **Big plants (trees, shrubs and perennials)**
5. **Little plants (annual flowers)**

Of course, the guidelines above are just guidelines. You may not be able to afford the deck right away, but you could put a fountain in or a couple of trees while you're waiting to win the lottery.

Making a work calendar

After you have the overall plan for your garden worked out, divide the plan into stages, including what you want to do this year, what you want to do next year, and then everything else. (Next year, you can figure out what to do for the following year or two, and so on.) Be flexible. Sometimes creating the garden of your dreams takes longer than you think. Don't try to fit too much into any particular year or season, or you'll burn out long before your garden is finished.

Feng Shui is all about balance and harmony, and one of the things you need to balance is your time, money and energy!

The longest journey starts with a single step. Start with a small step and you eventually reach your garden goals.

After you've settled on what needs to be done this year, break the work into seasons, deciding on what can be done when. You'll be busiest with gardening tasks in the spring and fall, so keep that in mind as you plan your projects.

If you already have a garden established, and you're just changing some things around, you still need to weed while you're installing the pond. Keep that in mind as you make your work schedule.

If you're an experienced gardener, you have a pretty good idea of what you have to do from season to season. If you're new at the game, then find out what you have to do when in your particular climate. In milder climates, for example, gladioli bulbs can be left in the ground. In colder zones, they have to be dug up every fall. Knowing this info helps you plan what you can do when in your garden. (And whether you want to mess around with gladioli.)

Finding gardening time

Who has time to garden? What with the kids, the job, the after-school sports? A low-maintenance garden doesn't have to take more than an hour or two a week to keep up, even during the height of gardening season (and in the winter it requires even less time.) But gardening is such a nice way to get in touch with nature and such a nice way to reduce stress that you should really give your best effort to finding time to garden. Besides, a good-looking garden is a joy to spend time in. Try these tips to shoehorn some extra time into your schedule:

- Enlist the kids and the spouse in planning the garden. If they feel part of it, they're more likely to help out with the chores later on.
- Spend a few minutes each week drawing up a list of gardening tasks to be done. Choose one task to do each week. Focus on doing that one task. You can accomplish a lot more if your energy isn't scattered. (You start cleaning up the leaves only to stop when you see the garden hose hasn't been put away for the winter, and you get halfway to the garage with the hose when you see that a rock has fallen from the retaining wall so you . . . don't get anything done, and two hours have passed.)
- Create a gardening co-op. Alternate Saturdays working in the gardens of a few close friends. Everyone pitches in to do what needs to be done. Working with others is a lot more fun than working alone, and more can be accomplished.
- You may even find that after you start finding the time to garden that you love it so much you're willing to give up television to do it.

Loving Low-Maintenance Gardening

You can achieve a beautiful Feng Shui garden even if you don't have a lot of time to devote to gardening. Keeping a garden low maintenance is easy if you plan ahead of time and keep up with chores so they don't get out of hand (turning a one-hour chore into a ten-hour chore). For instance, you can pull small weeds from your front flowerbed once a week or you can skip it and end up spending an entire weekend in July hacking through a jungle sized weedpatch where you can barely see your plants.

As you plan your garden, determine how much maintenance each type of plant needs. For example, a tree might require pruning, leaf cleanup, and mulching. A garden shed might need annual painting or a deck might need annual sealing. Factor these time demands into your garden planning.

A large lawn obviously takes a lot of time to mow, edge, and trim, so if you can limit the amount of lawn (and keep it in a regular shape, like a square or rectangle), you spend less time mowing. See Chapter 8 for ideas on creating smaller lawns.

Choosing carefree plants

If you plan on planting only those plants (try saying that ten times fast) that thrive in your environment, you have fewer gardening chores to keep up with. Remember these tips for easier caretaking:

- After a native plant has been established in your garden (a year or two), you don't need to water it. (Or at least, not very often.) So choose drought-tolerant native plants and dump the garden hose.
- Substitute ground cover for grass, particularly in those areas where you have difficulty getting grass to grow.
- Eliminate plants that are susceptible to pests and diseases in your area. Check with your local extension agency.
- Even though annuals are replaced, um, annually, choose those that work best in your area to reduce maintenance.
- Shrubs can be low maintenance if you choose healthy, native plants.

- Choose plants that produce less litter. Crab apple trees create crab apples, and someone has to pick them up (or, if that someone is a kid, throw them at passersby). Pinecones may make festive centerpieces, but again, someone has to collect them. Choose trees with small leaves (less raking) and avoid fruit trees to save on maintenance.

Selecting simple garden structures

Keep your garden structures low maintenance, too. This reduces the amount of time you spend repairing, painting, and replacing objects in your garden. Here's how:

- **Don't paint or stain garden structures.** Naturally weathered wood looks good and doesn't require much upkeep.

  One pair of gardeners bought a certain house largely because of the huge deck in back, on which they envisioned hosting lots of parties. Well, they got to host their parties, but they didn't love it so much when they realized the original homeowners had painted the deck and now they had to re-paint it every year or it looked terrible!
- **Choose dark-colored wrought-iron furniture for low-maintenance tables and chairs.**
- **Install a self-contained fountain or birdbath rather than a pond**. Ponds require much more maintenance and are more difficult to install.

Growing a garden with minimal effort

If you've chosen suitable plants and have reduced maintenance time on sheds, furniture, and other garden structures, you're well on your way to keeping gardening demands to a minimum.

Now, place the right plants in the right places, and you reduce maintenance needs even further! For example

- **Create beds of plants.** Don't mow and trim around four different beds if you can mow and trim around one (albeit a big one).
- **Group like plants together.** Plants that need like amounts of water, for example, can be placed together to reduce maintenance time.

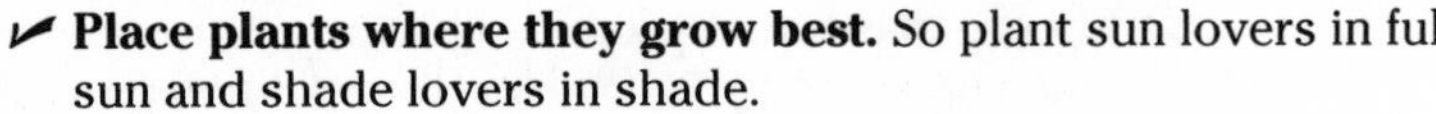

- **Place plants where they grow best.** So plant sun lovers in full sun and shade lovers in shade.

- **Avoid unnecessary pruning by knowing how big a specific plant grows and planting it where it has room to reach its full potential.** Tomorrow comes sooner than you think. Consider the case of the gardener who planted a pin oak as a sapling when he first purchased his house. His wife said, "You're planting that too close to the house, aren't you?" and he said, "It'll be 25 years before we have to worry about that." Well, before he knew it, he was chopping down that pin oak because it was dropping branches on the roof. Remember, conscious and deliberate placement and planning are important in Feng Shui. A Feng Shui garden isn't meant to be enjoyed for just one season but for many years to come.
- **Keep more delicate plants in containers.** That way, you can simply bring them indoors instead of having to create elaborate protective measures for delicate plants in the ground.
- **Prioritize maintenance jobs.** Make sure that the most important jobs — the ones most beneficial to your plants — get done. The others can wait.

High-Octane Gardening: For Serious Gardeners Only

If you've just flipped through the first few pages of this chapter saying, "What kinda wimp wants a low-maintenance garden?" then this section is for you.

If you love gardening, then you may want to kick it up a notch and turn your hand to higher-maintenance gardening. We've got you covered.

Fiddling with fun exotics

If you don't mind a little extra work, try adding some exotic plants to your garden. These plants look gorgeous and create a stunning atmosphere for you and your guests, but they aren't as easy to live with as native plants.

For example, if you live in Minnesota, you can put some potted palms and bougainvillea on the patio. Of course, you can only keep them outside for about three weeks in summer, but during those three weeks you can pretend you're in the Bahamas!

Exotic plants make a terrific focal point in the summer — they really generate some good chi — but they may require extra protection in winter.

Some exotics, such as the following, can tolerate a bit of cold and a nip of frost:

- Bamboo (very auspicious in Feng Shui)
- Cattleya orchids
- Lily hybrids
- Moonflower
- Ornamental rhubarb
- Painted nettle
- Rose moss
- Spider flower
- Yucca

Planning projects over the long haul

Serious gardeners always have more plans for their garden than they have garden to try the plans out on. But if you're a high-octane gardener, then go ahead and reach for the stars. Don't let naysayers, like the county extension agent, try to talk you out of it.

- Investigate different types of flowers, vegetables, shrubs, trees, and vines. Use your imagination — if you want red, white, and blue potatoes for your Fourth of July potato salad, you can find potato hybrids in each of those colors.
- During the wintertime, order seed catalogs from every mail-order garden supply shop that you can find (thank goodness for the Internet!). Imagine planting an orchard of nut trees. Imagine cultivating your own vineyard. Then make it happen.
- Try out some fun and interesting plants that take time to cultivate. Asparagus doesn't produce in its first year. Many plants take a couple years to reach their full glory. So order them up, but plan on reaping what you sow a little later than usual.

Experimenting requires sacrifice. Accept that some of those plants aren't going to work out and they're going to have to go. Stick them in the compost bin after thanking them for giving it a try.

Preventing gardening burnout

In the cold dark days of winter, you may think you want to spend the entire spring in the garden, but when spring rolls around, you may find that you want to do a little something else now and then, like sleep. Feng Shui is about balance, remember?

High-octane gardeners have to guard against burnout. They may start out in a blaze of glory, but by midsummer, they're wishing they didn't have to spend four hours a day in the garden chopping the weeds down.

The best advice we can give is to start in stages. Add a couple of higher maintenance exotics to your existing garden. Begin one larger project, such as planting a few trees in that orchard, but don't try to do it all in one go.

To get a grip on how long it will actually take to see your garden dreams come true, create a step-by-step plan that details what needs to be done. Include items like, "Buy the trees," which may take more than ten minutes, and "Prepare the soil," which may take an entire weekend. Add up the various items, calculating how long you think you'll spend on each and then double the estimate (we're not kidding.) If you estimate that doing your project will take 160 hours, realize that that is the equivalent of a month's worth of full-time work. How and when will you be able to do it? (See the section, "Making a work calendar" earlier in this chapter for more information on planning.)

You want to experiment with fun new ideas in your garden but still be realistic about how much time and energy you need to set aside. That way you can enjoy your gardening experience more.

Part III

Harvesting the Blessings of Feng Shui

"By observing the dragon of the East, the tiger of the West, the turtle of the North, and the phoenix of the South, I hope to neutralize the effects of the weasel across the street and the junkyard dog next door."

In this part . . .

Break out the shovels and hoes. In this part, we show you how to choose Feng Shui plants for your garden, how to raise the chi by attracting wildlife, and how to spot Feng Shui challenges. We give you the fixes you need to cure common Feng Shui problems, such as depressed energy, stagnant chi, and out-of-balance Elements. You can pick up pointers on using simple cures — light, color, sound, and more — to raise (enhance) the chi everywhere in your garden.

Chapter 10

Choosing Plants for Your Garden

In This Chapter

- Using plants to increase the chi in your garden
- Figuring out which plants to avoid

You have a shelf full of gardening books open on the table in front of you and you're ready to start ordering seeds and bulbs. Problem is, which ones should you order? They all look pretty nice, don't they? Why not one of each?

A Feng Shui garden contains carefully selected trees, shrubs, plants, and flowers. Closing your eyes and pointing doesn't do it! Choosing the right plants for your garden goes a long way toward creating a welcoming, inviting garden spot — perfect Feng Shui! And plants that work in your environment and suit your temperament and energy level reward you with a more successful garden.

In this chapter, we show you how to select the right plants for your garden to elevate the chi and make your garden a welcoming, enjoyable place to enter. We let you know which plants you may be better off avoiding and how to use plants that may have Feng Shui drawbacks.

Creating Good Chi with Friendly Plants

Plants create good living energy. They enhance the chi in your garden just by existing. Plus they make you feel good — they feed your soul, not to mention your stomach. Picking the right plants for your Feng Shui garden raises the positive energy level in your garden and in your life.

Although some plants are more Feng Shui–friendly than others, the most important consideration is what you like and what works well in your area. In general, an auspicious Feng Shui plant has rounded leaves instead of sharp, pointed ones (which can create negative, cutting chi), no thorns or spikes (again, this can create cutting chi), is perfectly healthy (dead or unhealthy plants create negative chi), and full of foliage or blossoms (spiky and spindly plants can create negative, cutting chi).

To pick plants that will raise the chi in your garden, combine personal inclination with the principles of Feng Shui. If you're the type of person who walks into a nursery and announces, "I want one of everything," we commend your enthusiasm but have to caution you to avoid overdoing it.

To create your perfect Feng Shui garden, select each plant for a reason — because you like its color or fragrance or simply because you can't imagine gardening without it.

Planting healthy native plants

Only hardy, healthy plants should find a place in your garden. Although you may be tempted to stop by the nearest discount store for this year's crop of annuals, remember that such plants may be stressed, cared for by people who don't know much about plants, or full of bugs, diseases, and other icky problems.

Choose plants from a well-respected source. Many nurseries and garden supply stores guarantee their plants and sell only fungus-, pest-, and disease-free plants — the plants you want in your garden.

Because native plants are resistant to native pests and tolerate native climate conditions best, choose plants local to your area. Among other things, they don't import exotic diseases into your vegetable plot!

Don't force a plant that loves the warm summer sun to survive in frigid northern climates. It may live, but it probably won't thrive. Mediocre and sick plants depress the chi in your garden. Instead, choose only those plants that thrive in your *climate zone* (U.S. Department of Agriculture-identified regions that share similar weather patterns, including average low and high temperatures).

If you don't know your climate zone, check the USDA Plant Hardiness Zone guide at `www.usda.gov`.

Overgrown, dying, and dead plants are poor Feng Shui. They depress the chi in the garden, and they're not very beautiful to look at! Remove such plants and put them in the compost pile, where they will eventually be returned to Mother Earth.

Following Feng Shui principles

A Feng Shui garden is a garden in balance. It has some areas with flowers, shrubs, and trees. It has some areas of emptiness. In all cases, the plants can be seen and appreciated. They're not all cluttered together in a shapeless mass.

When you choose plants for your garden, remember to place the plants in their most auspicious locations in the Bagua. (See Chapters 3 and 6 for more information on the Bagua and planting according to the life sectors of the Bagua.) And don't forget to keep yin and yang energy in balance. (See Chapter 2 for more information about yin and yang.)

Use the color of plants to enhance the chi in each of the Life Sectors. For example, each of the following plants has flowers that enhance the chi in the sector I mention:

- Red poppies in the Fame sector
- Pink begonias in the Relationships sector
- White jasmine in the Children sector
- Silver rod in the Helpful People sector
- Dark blue lobelia in the Career sector
- Blue primroses in the Knowledge sector
- Green foliage in the Family sector
- Purple wisteria in the Wealth sector
- Yellow daffodils in the T'ai Chi sector

Of course, you can choose other plants according to your location, tastes, and what's available. Just try to choose plants of the appropriate color for each Life Sector.

Jayme Barrett, Feng Shui consultant and contributor to this book, says, "You want different shapes of plants in your garden. Create a variety for yin and yang energy. Choose some bushy plants, some upright plants, and some trailing plants to ensure a range of textures and looks to the space."

Saying it with plants

Different plants symbolize different meanings. Knowing these meanings can help you pick plants that enhance your garden.

- Bamboo = good health and longevity
- Chrysanthemum = resolution and fortitude
- Cypress = nobility
- Fruit trees = abundance
- Gardenia = strength
- Orange tree = good fortune
- Orchid = longevity
- Peach tree = immortality
- Peony = wealth
- Pine = faithfulness

To keep yin/yang energy in balance, remember the following:

- All living things have yang energy, but plain foliage seems less energetic than bright blossoms. Keep a nice contrast between bunches of blossoming flowers and shades of foliage in a range of greens.
- Keep areas of open space to alternate with planted areas.
- Boulders, stone, and rocks give off yang energy; water features give off yin energy, unless they're running, in which case they may bring moving energy (yang) into the garden.

Considering Plants to Use with Caution

Some plants, no matter how healthy and alive they are, generate negative chi. Something about them feels threatening (or actually *is* threatening).

For example, Feng Shui gardeners avoid poisonous plants because they're subtly threatening — and they can be toxic to the wildlife you want to entice into your garden (and toxic to you).

Some plants may seem threatening on a subtle, energetic level if they're not treated appropriately in the garden. Use care when including such plants in your garden.

Thorny plants

Roses, bougainvillea, and other plants that have thorns may be beautiful to look at and to smell, but those sharp thorns can generate negative, stabbing chi. Some Feng Shui gardeners avoid thorny plants entirely.

If you do want to use them in your garden, be careful. For example, a bougainvillea draped on an archway may look gorgeous, but if the thorns snag your clothing or your skin as you walk through the archway, you're not going to feel very welcome in the garden! Keep the following suggestion in mind when considering thorny plants in your Feng Shui garden:

- Set thorny plants well away from entrances and walkways.
- Keep the thorns from pointing directly at people to avoid negative chi from "stabbing" them. You can "shield" people by planting other flowers around the roses.
- Thorny plants and shrubs placed on the perimeter of your garden can actually serve the useful purpose of keeping some pests out of the garden, such as the neighbor's dog.
- Select thornless varieties when possible. Some roses come in thornless versions, for example.

Spiny plants

Like thorny plants, spiny cacti are often avoided in a Feng Shui garden because the spikes seem threatening and can create negative arrows of chi. Just looking at them makes your fingers hurt! If you want to include cacti in your garden (particularly if they're appropriate for your region), try the following suggestions:

- Avoid cacti with mammoth spines. No matter what you do, these cacti may always seem threatening to visitors.
- Choose succulents (cacti-like plants) with small, subtle scales or spines.
- Keep cacti out of traveled areas — pathways, entrances.

Clinically depressed plants

You may want to avoid plants that droop downward or appear sad, like the weeping willow. They can depress the energy of a garden. However, if you happen to love a particular droopy plant, try to

- Lift the energy of trailing plants by wrapping them around trellises or other structures.
- Keep trailing vines from encroaching on pathways — stepping on plants makes people feel bad, and they may trip over them (a lawsuit from a visitor may make you as clinically depressed as the weeping willow).

Climbing plants

Climbers can brighten up all sorts of garden spaces — porches and patios and enclosed courtyards. Some of the more aggressive climbers, such as ivy, can damage structures, though; so be careful in your choices. Grow climbers on trellises rather than walls to protect your property.

Also, when you use climbing plants in the garden, make sure that outdoor furniture is set away from the plants. Visitors may not like the feel of leaves brushing their necks, and they're probably going to feel subtly negative about fronds that seem to reach out and touch them.

Hanging plants

To lift the eye and the chi in the garden, hang baskets of plants, or train plants to grow over archways, gazebos, and pergolas. But use special care.

Hanging objects can seem subtly threatening to people (so this caution goes for anything you may hang in your garden, such as wind chimes). Visitors may have the sense that the plant is going to fall on them — they may not even realize that they have that sense, but their bodies are aware of it on an energetic level. If you hang baskets around your garden, keep the following suggestions in mind:

- Keep hanging baskets securely fastened to the roof or wall. In bad weather, take them indoors or place them in a sheltered area so the baskets aren't damaged.
- Don't place seats beneath hanging plants. The chair's occupant may feel threatened.
- Place furniture so that hanging plants don't obscure the view as people relax in the garden or chat with one another.
- Hang baskets high enough so that guests don't bump into them as they move around the garden.

Chapter 11

Attracting Wildlife to Enhance Good Chi

In This Chapter

- Understanding why you want the birds and the bees
- Enticing animals into your garden
- Establishing a wildlife refuge in your backyard

Living creatures create living energy, according to the principles of Feng Shui. So you could say that animals give off good vibes — at least when you're not swatting at them with a rolled-up newspaper. This living energy enhances and balances the chi in your garden (and chi, which is the energy the universe creates, is the source of abundance in your garden and in your life.) In other words, one small rat terrier can ensure a pleasantly prosperous life!

Pets aren't the only living creatures that can raise the chi in your environment, though. Feng Shui encourages the natural approach to design and placement, and what could be more natural than a squirrel or two in the garden? Wildlife, including birds, insects, and mammals, can also enhance chi and add the beauty of nature to your garden.

In this chapter, you find out how to attract different types of wildlife to your garden in order to balance and improve chi. You also discover some tips for avoiding unfavorable (not to mention unpleasant) wildlife, and how to keep the deer out of the vegetable patch without resorting to drastic measures.

Attracting Birds to Your Garden

Ahh, the sweet sound of a lark! What could be more pleasant on a summer day? (Okay, besides a cold brewski?) In fact, sound raises the chi in your garden, which is why Feng Shui gardens often have wind chimes and other music makers in them. (See Chapter 12 for more information on the role of sound in Feng Shui.)

Birds not only provide an attractive visual and auditory treat when they visit your garden, but they also eat insects, such as mosquitoes, that cause problems for people (and their plants). Attracting birds, especially to an area of the garden that may have problems with slow-moving or stagnant chi, helps the chi move more freely throughout the space. (See Chapters 1 and 2 for more information on the movement of chi.)

At least one Feng Shui practitioner keeps a peacock in her garden. Not only does the bird bring living chi into the garden, but it's also a beautiful sight to behold.

Birdbaths can be an attractive Water element in your garden that encourages birds to visit. But be sure to keep the water (and the birdbath itself) clean. Stagnant water is very bad Feng Shui anywhere in the home or garden and encourages mosquito breeding, so consider opting for a birdbath with a fountain because the water is active and circulating. To clean a birdbath, dump the water out regularly and refill. (You can bail it out with cups or a siphon if your birdbath is too heavy to lift and dump.) See Chapter 4 for more information on water features in the garden.

Keeping the birdies well fed

To attract a variety of birds to your garden, you need to create diversity in your garden. As you plan, think of the different foods that birds eat: insects, fruit, seeds, and nuts. Ask yourself how you can provide these meals to the birds that you want in your garden.

Here are some tips to attract birds to your garden:

- Supply fruit by planting shrubs that produce berries and letting the pear tree go to the birds.
- Contribute insects by planting flowers that attract them (more on inviting insects into your garden in the section "Inviting Butterflies and Bugs" later in this chapter).
- Purchase seeds and nuts at the grocery store or the pet store during the lean winter months. In fact, you can purchase *insects* from the pet store, too, but that may be taking it a step too far. A general rule is to let birds find their own crickets.

See the section "Placing bird feeders" later in the chapter for more on feeding our feathered friends.

All the Five Elements (see Chapter 3) are present and balanced in the fabulous Feng Shui garden. The pool adds the Water element, the stones add the Earth element, the plants add the Wood element, the patio chairs add Metal, and the grill in that area adds Fire.

©2004 EDAW — photography by Dixi Carrillo

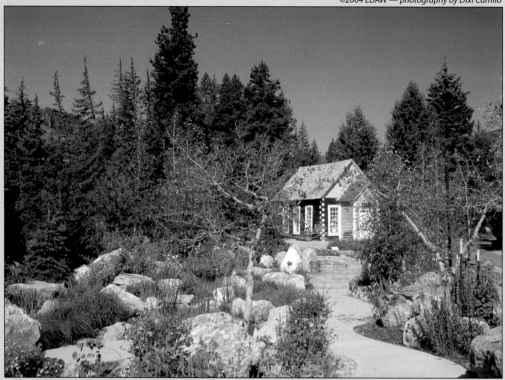

An attractive curving path prevents chi from rushing toward the house.

Photo courtesy of author

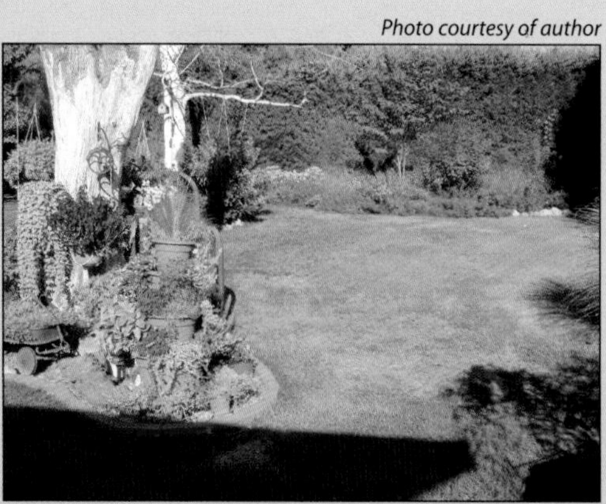

Groups of plants in an open space keep the chi from moving too fast.

Photo courtesy of author

Planting on different levels keeps the chi from stagnating.

The curved beds and round-shaped plants help reduce cutting chi (see Chapter 4) from the corners of the house.

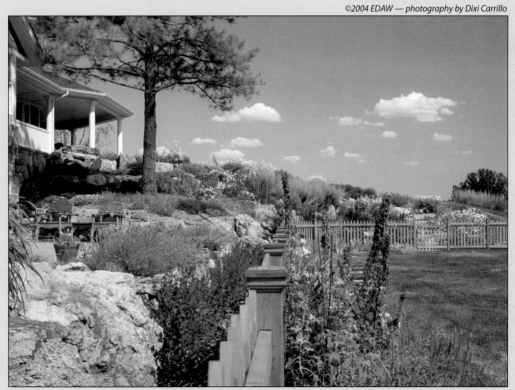

The fence helps support this garden and keeps the chi from leaving down the slope of the yard.

When used properly, a water feature, such as a waterfall into a pond, equals excellent Feng Shui because moving water represents abundance coming into your life. Goldfish in the pond are also auspicious.

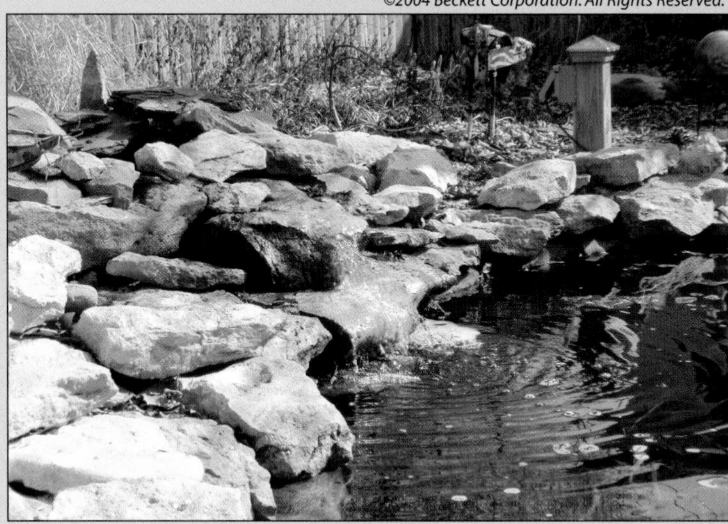

Your Feng Shui garden should be as attractive and inviting as possible all year long. A water feature keeps this fall garden looking great, even though many of the plants are no longer in bloom. (Chapter 8 discusses preparing your garden for all seasons.)

If waterfalls aren't your thing, you can still get the Feng Shui benefits of a water feature by selecting one that suits your tastes.

Varieties of plants and shrubs keep yin and yang energy in balance.

The Earth element of the stone terrace helps balance the wood element of the plants.

The dense plantings of this entertainment area, along with the activity that happens here, is balanced with the quiet open area farther out in the garden.

©2004 EDAW — photography by Dixi Carrillo

©2004 EDAW — photography by Dixi Carrillo

Archways are a popular feature in Feng Shui gardens because they serve as the Mouth of Chi (see Chapter 4) and add height and visual interest to attract visitors. They also frame the garden beyond them and invite visitors to move forward.

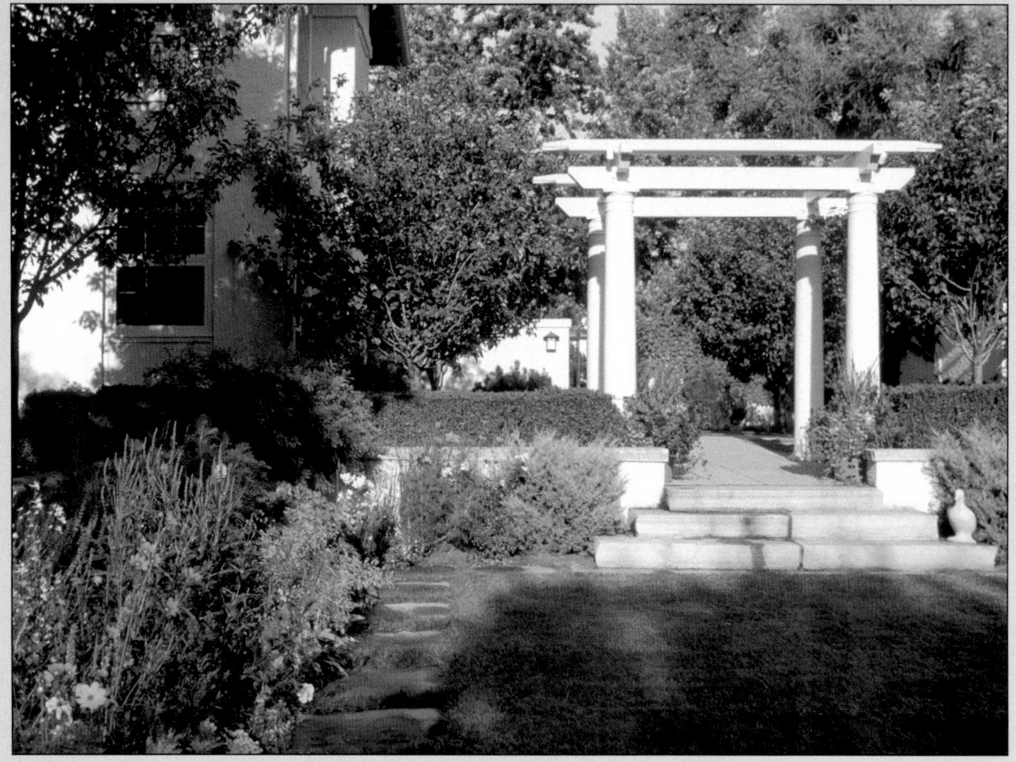

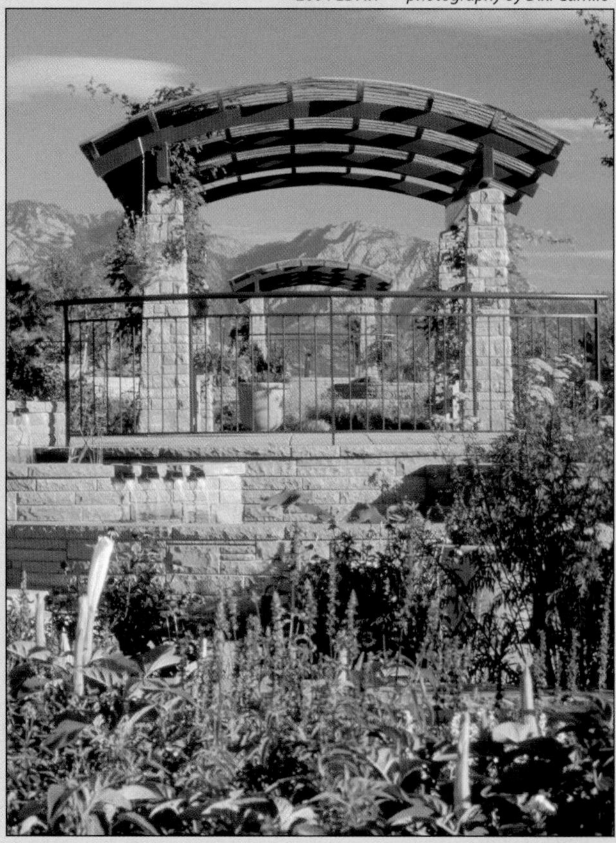

You don't need a large private yard to enjoy a Feng Shui garden. This shared garden (above) for a large apartment complex brings positive chi to everyone who lives there. If you do happen to have a small space of your own, the photo below should provide some fun inspiration. (Chapter 19 also provides great tips for gardening in small and common spaces.)

A nontraditional garden, such as this one, can incorporate Feng Shui principles just as easily as a traditional one. Notice the gently curving beds and walkways to allow smooth chi flow. Also notice how all the Five Elements are balanced and present.

Hummingbirds are attracted to the color red, which is a favorable color in Feng Shui. If you want to attract these lovely little birds, a bed of red (or orange, pink, or purple) flowers will do the trick. Think daylilies, geraniums, and phlox in the appropriate hues. Your local gardening store can help you determine which plants are available and appropriate for your region's gardening conditions. See Chapter 13 for creating a hummingbird-themed garden.

If you want to appeal to sparrows and finches, they love native grasses and herbaceous plants — think sunflowers, goldenrods, and asters. If you prefer blue jays and bluebirds, they're partial to berry-producing shrubs, such as winterberry.

Keep a journal of the bird species you see in your garden. Use a field guide to help you identify the birds you don't immediately recognize. Find out more about the species native to your area and plan which plants will encourage them to visit your garden. To brush up on your bird knowledge, pick up a copy of *Bird Watching For Dummies,* by Bill Thompson, III (Wiley Publishing, Inc.).

Birds pick insects directly off foliage and stems (with the exception of the wily woodpecker, which actually digs into trees to find its tasty snack of spiders and larvae). To encourage birds to visit your garden, avoid using insecticides. Take a look at Chapter 7 for ways to keep out bugs that you don't want in the garden.

Some birds hop along the ground scrounging through leaf litter for insects. In that case, a perfectly raked and manicured lawn prevents them from filling up on ants and other crawlers. If you don't want dead leaves littering your lawn, consider providing natural, untreated mulch under trees and shrubs to benefit these walkin' robins. You can find mulch at any of your local gardening stores and at discount stores, such as Wal-Mart or K-Mart.

Birds have natural predators, including birds that eat other birds (hawks, for example). Needless to say, dead birds in the garden don't represent good Feng Shui. Dispose of the carcasses carefully: Wear gloves and follow local regulations for discarding dead animals. The local humane society or your neighborhood vet can tell you what these regulations are. Also, don't allow your pets to roll in them or chew on them because the dead birds may carry diseases.

Using birdhouses

Is your garden a nice place to visit but not a place a bird would want to live? You can correct this problem by providing your winged guests with birdhouses and nesting boxes (simple wooden boxes with a floor and four sides where birds can build nests). You can wedge birdhouses between the trunk of the tree and a branch to welcome many busy mama birds in the summertime.

Some birds, like purple martins, happily nest inside dried and hollowed-out gourds that you can hang from a tree. Others take residence in regular, old-fashioned birdhouses, as long as they're clean and kept away from predators, such as cats. To keep your birdhouses out of the reach of predators, hang them from a branch or a post with a chain.

You can find birdhouses at gardening stores, home improvement stores, and discount centers. Here's what to look for when purchasing a birdhouse:

- Choose a birdhouse that's cozy and roomy enough for a bird or two but not so large that an entire flock can fit inside.
- Look for a birdhouse with a small peg that extends just beneath the entrance to the birdhouse so the mama bird can inspect the interior of the house before moving in.
- Make sure that the entrance is just the width of a grown bird. If the opening is too large, you're asking for the invasion of the body-snatchers (also known as squirrels).
- Seek a birdhouse with a natural look — unpainted and unembellished. Birds are more attracted to this look, and birdhouses that have a natural look are less likely to be toxic than painted birdhouses.
- Select wooden birdhouses. Birds prefer wooden homes because wood is what they're accustomed to building their homes in.

If you're truly ambitious, you can purchase a birdhouse kit to make (again, from a garden or home improvement store) or find a pattern and materials at a lumberyard or woodworking shop and make one from scratch. As long as you're patient, this endeavor can be a fun springtime project for you and your kids.

The birdhouse is part of the design of your garden. Integrate it well with other objects in your garden, and it will be a good example of Feng Shui. In other words, don't install a birdhouse with a lot of sharp corners, and don't pick a birdhouse you think is ugly. Your birdhouse can represent Wood element, and by creating birdhouses of different shapes, you can enhance the other Five Elements in your garden.

Placing bird feeders

In the spring and summer months, an abundant garden yields an all-you-can-eat buffet of caterpillars and plant seeds for birds. But don't forget about your feathered friends during the winter months! To keep the birds in your garden healthy (and alive), place bird feeders throughout your garden.

Keep in mind that different birds have different needs. Hummingbirds need sugary water in specially-designed hummingbird feeders. (They need these special feeders so your garden isn't overrun by ants attracted to the smell of sugar.) For details on how to make sugar water, see Chapter 14. Other birds prefer sunflower seeds or *millet* (a type of cereal grain). You can provide birds with needed fats and carbohydrates by adding *suet* (solid fat, either animal or vegetable) or peanut butter to the seed mix.

Inviting Butterflies and Bugs

Nothing matches a summer morning watching the butterflies in your garden, except maybe watching your neighbor do yardwork while you're lounging in the hammock.

Many insects serve a useful purpose in your garden. All living creatures create living energy, or chi, which brings abundance to you! Some insects pollinate your plants. Earthworms and ants aerate the soil. Ground beetles eat slugs. Other insects are food for the birds that you may want in your garden. Still other insects feed on the insects that can be destructive to your garden.

Beneficial bugs: They're out there

You can find information on creating a butterfly-themed garden in Chapter 14. But butterflies aren't the only insects you may want to invite to the party. To attract other beneficial bugs, such as ladybugs and spiders (yes, spiders are good for your garden) remember that they all need food, water, shelter, and nesting sites.

Avoid using inorganic pesticides if you want to attract insects to your garden. Otherwise, you fumigate the good insects along with the bad.

To keep insects coming back for more, plan your garden so that flowers are always blossoming — it doesn't have to be the same kind of flower doing all the work. Consider

- Planting daffodils, irises, and tulips for the insects in early spring.
- Putting in perennials like peonies and phlox that bloom a bit later in the spring.
- Using grasses and other herbaceous plants and blossoming annuals and perennials such as day lilies, impatiens, moss roses, and bee balm for summer pollinators.
- Perennials like asters and mums that can provide food in later summer and early fall for the insects that haven't flown the coop.

In order to ensure harmony and the free flow of chi in your garden, balance the types of plants you choose so that the Five Elements of Feng Shui are represented. Don't choose plants that are all one color or size. See Chapter 10 for more information on choosing Feng Shui plants for your garden.

Discouraging unfavorable bugs

Some bugs aren't good for your garden (or for you). Mosquitoes carry dangerous diseases, such as the West Nile virus. Aphids destroy plants. And other insects have equally bad habits — they sting and bite for no good reason. But before you reach for pesticide — which kills the good insects along with the bad — consider some other ways of discouraging unfavorable bugs:

- Eliminate standing or stagnant water. If you have a pond, install a circulating pump (with a good bio-filter to keep the gunk out) to keep the water moving.
- Landscape your yard so pools of water don't collect after a rain. To ensure good runoff from your yard, you may have to bring in more soil and re-sod.
- Bugs hate the smell of citronella, so invest in torches or candles that give off the smell. You can find these candles and torches at any home-improvement store.
- Insects such as ladybugs and some types of flies eat aphids (which destroy plants). You can purchase ladybugs to put in your garden from some nurseries and mail-order sources.
- Keep your garden diverse. Doing so helps keep the producer-consumer cycle in balance so that no one thing (such as unfavorable bugs) takes over the garden.
- Watch for signs of stressed plants, which are attractive to bugs (and diseases). Too much or too little sunlight or

water contributes to plant stress. Remove diseased or dead leaves and branches.

- Keep up with the weeding!
- Remove mulch if too many insects burrow in it.
- Try mechanical devices such as traps, cages, and barriers. Or putting flypaper on trees can spell the end to many bugs.
- Put up a bat house (bats dine on their body weight in insects every night!)
- If you must resort to pesticides, use them carefully and sparingly and choose organic versions.
- Accept a few pesky bugs as food for the birds!

Bringing Mammals into the Garden

Most gardeners spend their time trying to get mammals *out* of the garden, because nothing can destroy months of hard work quite like a sweet bunny rabbit and all her children. But sometimes you want to see a little furry creature hopping along in your garden. Mammals, like birds and insects, need food, water, shelter, and nesting sites. Provide these, and you can have a virtual zoo in your backyard!

Some mammals, such as raccoons, can carry the rabies virus. You don't want to be bitten by a rabid animal (we're assuming), and you don't want your pets at risk, either (we're also assuming). So be cautious about approaching any wild animal — and be especially careful if the animal starts approaching you!

Understanding mammals

By understanding the habits of various mammals, you can figure out how to attract them to your garden. (Studying the habits of mammals native to your environment is a good project for a bored family on a rainy afternoon.) Consider the following to get you started:

- Shrews (the rodent variety, not the next-door neighbor type) like leaf litter and eat twice their body weight in insects every day.
- Mice feed on plants, seeds, nuts, and insects.
- Rabbits like grasses and other herbaceous plants, plus bark and twigs.

- Squirrels eat acorns and beechnuts and help trees reproduce. They also enjoy berries from berry-producing shrubs.
- Raccoons like hollow trees and crevices between rocks and fallen logs as shelter.
- Deer like woody plants and shrubs. They eat grass and flowers as well. Providing apples or other fruits at an accessible level brings them to your garden. (If you live in a suburban neighborhood, you may want to check with the neighbors first.)
- Coyotes eat almost any animal (and even some large insects).
- Red foxes like corn, berries, and fruits.

Wildlife attracts wildlife. If you have pets, they may attract predators, depending on where you live. We've heard stories of outdoor cats and small dogs being carted off by hawks and owls, and mountain lions and coyotes getting into tangles with dogs. Bears can also be a danger. People in rural areas need to be aware.

Understanding the life cycle

Nature stays in balance because of the life cycle of living things. A seed is planted, and a flower grows, blooms, and eventually dies. Or, the flower may be eaten. Being eaten measures largely into the life cycle of most living things. When a plant is eaten, it rarely upsets anyone, but when a hawk swoops down on an unsuspecting rabbit, even a veteran outdoorsman may get a little pale.

The life cycle ensures that no species becomes too dominant in its environment; if one species does become too dominant, the animal can destroy its own habitat. Think of a pond covered with algae: It's a dying habitat, all because the algae grew too dominant. A lot of work is required to correct an overgrown algae problem. Similarly, if one species becomes too dominant in your garden, you have to spend time, money, and effort returning the garden to its natural balance. See the section "Balancing act: When one species gets out of hand," later in this chapter for more information on what to do if one species gets out of hand in your garden.

Oh, Deer! What to do with too many mammals?

You imagined yourself sipping a cup of tea on your back porch while watching a doe drink from the pond on the edge of your property. What you didn't expect was having an entire herd of deer in your backyard rooting up the rosebushes. What should you do?

Don't fence me in — or, actually, do

Fences and other barriers are the best protection against mammals. If deer are a problem, experts recommend an 8-foot fence because deer can jump really, really high (however, many housing developments prohibit fences taller than 6 feet, so check before you install a fence). If you can't build an 8-foot fence, remember that deer need a clear landing space, so planting shrubs or a hedge inside the fence will discourage them from jumping.

Wood fences make an attractive option. Being made of natural materials, they represent the Wood element and are a good example of Feng Shui. You can also use wire mesh, although this option is less appropriate for Feng Shui. (However, practical needs take precedence over Feng Shui needs.)

Barbed wire causes injuries to people, pets, and wildlife — so don't use it. Using barbed wire is also bad Feng Shui — the sharp barbs create negative arrows of chi energy.

Because some animals try to burrow under fences (the irresistible aroma of your garden may lure them), make certain that the fence extends 6 inches or so into the ground. A lip that extends outward at the base of the fence can also keep mammals from burrowing under the fence.

Caging your plants

You can protect your plants by installing cages around them. Plant cages can be purchased at most nurseries. Consult with the salesperson or your local extension agent to find out which cages work best in your environment, based on the typical pests in your area. Use the following equipment to ensure that your plants have a long life:

- **Wire mesh cages:** Surround your tree trunks and plant stems with wire mesh cages to prevent mammals from gnawing on them. For deer, the cage should be about 5 feet high.
- **Wire baskets:** Plant bulbs and other perennials inside wire baskets or in an old coffee can punched with drainage holes to prevent moles and other burrowers from chewing up your tulips before they have the chance to bloom.
- **Plastic netting:** Cover fruit trees and favored vegetables with plastic netting to discourage birds and small mammals from harvesting your crop for you.

Repelling all boarders

Sometimes cages may not be enough to prevent pesky pests from munching on your plants. You may need to resort to other tactics to discourage them. Try the following:

- **Sprays:** You can repel some animals by spraying plants with a combination of red pepper and dishwasher soap. The pungent aroma of this recipe turns animals away from your turnips. Your local extension service (check the local government listing in your phone book) or an organic nursery can tell you which repellents work best in your region.
- **Plants:** Use plants to repel mammals. The smell of plants such as wormwoods, onions, and marigolds drive rabbits and gophers off. Plant these flowers around vulnerable plants to prevent the mammals from getting to them.
- **Electronic pest repellers:** Electronic pest repellers that produce sounds that mammals (including humans) find unattractive may work, although you have to decide whether the noise pollution is worth it. (Incidentally, unpleasant noises are bad Feng Shui.) You can find these at most home improvement stores and at many nurseries.

Balancing act: When one species gets out of hand

Sometimes, your best-laid plans result in an overabundance of one type of animal and a shortfall of every other type of animal. For example, your attempts to attract bats to get rid of the mosquitoes has resulted in a backyard that no one wants to sit in after dark — except maybe the same people who love Alfred Hitchcock movies.

An ounce of prevention

What do you do? As in all things Feng Shui, prevention is the answer. Just as you balance the Five Elements so that no one element overwhelms the others, so, too, should you balance your wildlife attraction efforts so that more than one type of wildlife is attracted to your garden. When making plans to create a certain theme or attract a certain species to your garden, understand how this impacts the environment. A garden designed and planted to attract scads of hummingbirds, for example, is almost certain to also attract scads of honeybees. Consider this potential situation before creating the hummingbird garden — especially if you're allergic to bee stings.

In the planning stages, you can easily work out what to do to counteract the honeybee problem. (Or you can abandon the idea of creating a hummingbird garden, if you must.) Some other solutions may include setting up birdhouses and feeders to attract birds that eat honeybees. Or maybe you can create a rock garden that attracts lizards that eat honeybees. Just remember that every action creates a consequence, and don't let the consequences take you by surprise.

A pound of cure

If it's too late to prevent an unbalanced garden, you need remedies that may, unfortunately, be time-consuming and expensive. See the section, "Oh, Deer! What to do with too many mammals?" earlier in this chapter for tips on keeping mammals in your garden under control.

Before taking the said time-consuming and expensive action, call your local extension service and explain your problem. Extension agents are familiar with gardens that have too many squirrels and not enough butterflies, and agents have advice for local conditions as well as suggestions for solving your overabundance problems. Some of the steps you can take may be very simple, such as replacing plastic and wood trash containers with metal containers that have locking lids. This strategy keeps the opossums and raccoons out of your garbage and your garden. Others may be more time-consuming and costly, such as erecting a tall privacy fence to keep out the deer.

Local nurseries and pest control companies also have plenty of experience dealing with local conditions. Remember that any creature that takes over a habitat becomes a pest. The label isn't restricted to rodents and flying insects.

When a garden is out of balance, time and dedication are necessary to restore the balance. Don't give up too soon and don't despair — you can set things right again.

Creating a Wildlife Refuge

You may want to create a wildlife refuge in order to protect animals whose habitat is quickly vanishing.

Making wildlife feel welcome in your garden on a regular basis takes a special effort. Animals must feel safe when they venture into your garden, which means that Fido yapping at the first tread of a hoof may eliminate your chances of creating a wildlife refuge.

If that's what you want, Honey

Think carefully about making your backyard into a wildlife refuge. Ask yourself why you want to have a wildlife refuge. If you truly love nature, have some experience with the outdoor life, and want to provide for wild creatures, those are good reasons to have a wildlife refuge. If you want a refuge because you think taming a white-tailed deer would be neat, umm, you should probably think again.

Creating a refuge takes time, effort, and possibly, some money. You need to research the wildlife in your particular location and how to support it. You need to decide what to do about injured and diseased animals that come your way — and you need to be capable of doing what needs to be done.

See the next section, "Supplying shelter from the storm," to get an idea of what goes into making a wildlife refuge.

Supplying shelter from the storm

Remember the key ingredients for attracting wildlife: food, water, shelter, and nesting sites. To create a wildlife refuge, you need to provide all of these to all the types of animals you hope to attract to your garden.

- **Water:** Water features are very good Feng Shui, and they're necessary to a wildlife refuge. A stream (natural or artificial) is perfect. A pond attracts frogs, toads, dragonflies, and even ducks. Running water discourages mosquitoes from breeding and doesn't freeze in the winter (frozen water is pretty useless for birds and other wildlife).
- **Food:** Nuts and berries are high on the list of foods that attract wildlife. Plant trees and berry-producing shrubs to attract mammals and birds. To attract bees, which are necessary to a refuge, plant tasty plants such as mint and black-eyed Susans. Brightly colored plants attract butterflies and other insects.
- **Shelter:** Shelter often doubles as a nesting site. Plant evergreen bushes in screens and groupings so that animals can take shelter in them. These evergreens give birds the nest-building materials they need. Woodpiles and leaf cover also provide shelter for many kinds of wildlife. Rocks and rock piles attract lizards, which sun themselves on the rock (lizards can't maintain their own body heat).

If you're interested in certifying your garden as a National Wildlife Habitat, check out the National Wildlife Federation at `www.nwf.org`.

Chapter 12

Making Your Garden More Feng Shui

In This Chapter

- Finding Feng Shui design problems in your garden
- Fixing Feng Shui problems

You've got a waterfall in your Fame sector, putting out the Fire element and depressing the chi in the garden. But you can't move the waterfall without hiring an expensive contractor. Uh-oh. Who you gonna call? The Feng Shui fixers, that's who.

Even if you planned your Feng Shui garden carefully, Feng Shui problems still crop up now and then. As all gardeners know, a garden is always in process. Sometimes you have to plant your seeds, and other times you have to harvest them. Sometimes you have to replace a dead plant or prune back a thriving one. Sometimes a structure you built falls down.

In this chapter, we describe Feng Shui fixes for common problems. These fixes, called *cures,* can remedy practically any problem related to the movement of chi in your garden (which is the source of most Feng Shui problems). Fixing Feng Shui design problems doesn't have to be difficult or costly. You can fix most problems (except those directly connected to location; see Chapter 5) using basic, easy-to-find, and easy-to-use cures. With just a few minutes of your time and some inexpensive objects, you can create a welcoming, warm environment that you and your guests can enjoy for all the seasons to come.

Just as you take care of routine garden maintenance on a regular basis, you may need to do routine Feng Shui maintenance in your garden. When one of the Five Elements starts getting a little out of balance, you need to take out the weed whacker and restore harmony.

Spotting and Solving Challenges

You've got your Feng Shui eyes (see Chapter 2) and your trusty Bagua (see Chapter 3), and you're ready, willing, and able to hunt for Feng Shui flaws in your garden. The question is: What are they and how do you spot them?

Most Feng Shui design problems crop up when chi can't move easily and freely throughout the garden (see Chapter 4). Problems also arise when the Five Elements (see Chapters 3 and 6) or the Life Sectors (see Chapter 3) are out of balance.

Chi is like a river that flows through your garden. If something in your garden blocks water from moving through it, then chances are high that chi is blocked also.

- If the energy in your garden seems either stagnant or too active, you've got a Feng Shui problem.
- If you try to use your contemplative spot and you end up feeling agitated and restless, your garden probably has too much active yang energy.
- If all your guests walk outside and immediately doze off in the chaise lounge, you have too much passive yin energy in your garden. (If they fall asleep on the brick patio floor, you've got a *real* problem. Or maybe you just had a really fun party.)
- Even if you simply feel less than terrific about walking into your garden, that can be a Feng Shui problem that needs to be cured. Feng Shui problems are often felt on a subtle, energetic level.

Evaluating your garden

You have to physically walk into your garden to evaluate it. (You can't do this evaluation by just using your imagination or delegating the job.) Move slowly and consciously through your garden, taking in the garden from a variety of directions and perspectives. Remember that paths go two ways, and walk each path in both directions.

Using your critical Feng Shui eyes

- **Notice if any cutting chi is being directed into the garden from outside or from objects and structures in the garden.** For example, make sure that no sharp or pointed leaves are jutting into your garden path or hanging over your hammock.

- **Visualize the flowing river of chi moving through your garden.** Can you see places where it gets stuck and stagnates, moves way too fast, or is sharp and cutting? Add cures to help the chi become healthier in those spots.

After you have your evaluation in hand, you can plan how to attack the Feng Shui challenges you've identified.

Clearing the clutter

The biggest stumbling block to the free movement of chi in the garden isn't some esoteric, little-known Feng Shui secret. The biggest stumbling block is . . . clutter. That's right. Junk. Too much junk prevents the chi from flowing smoothly and easily, thus messing with the energy in your garden. Plus, no one likes the sight of a bunch of overgrown plants tangled in a pile.

Jayme Barrett, who's a Feng Shui consultant and a contributor to this book, points out, "The backyard symbolizes your future. Clutter creates obstacles. So you're symbolically creating obstacles in your future if your backyard garden is cluttered." Ouch. Who wants to look into the future and see a bunch of overgrown, half-dead shrubs?

Also, you can't see and appreciate the beauty of nature if your garden is cluttered and clogged. Your garden shouldn't make you feel overworked and overwhelmed when you walk into it. Your garden should make you feel inspired and motivated.

Cutting back on overgrowth and undergrowth

Take a clear, hard, honest look at your garden and figure out what you (your spouse, the kids, the hired hand) need to do to return it to order.

Go ahead and

- Clear out the overgrowth and undergrowth.
- Weed flowerbeds and vegetable gardens.
- Prune back bushes and shrubs that have gotten out of control.
- Rake up leaves and other debris and keep mulch in good shape.

- Dig up plants that have outgrown their space and are encroaching on the territory of other plants.
- Create a small space between each plant so that each plant's beauty can be seen and appreciated, and so that each has room to grow. See Figure 12-1 for an example of appropriate spacing.
- Keep on a regular schedule so that clutter remains under control.

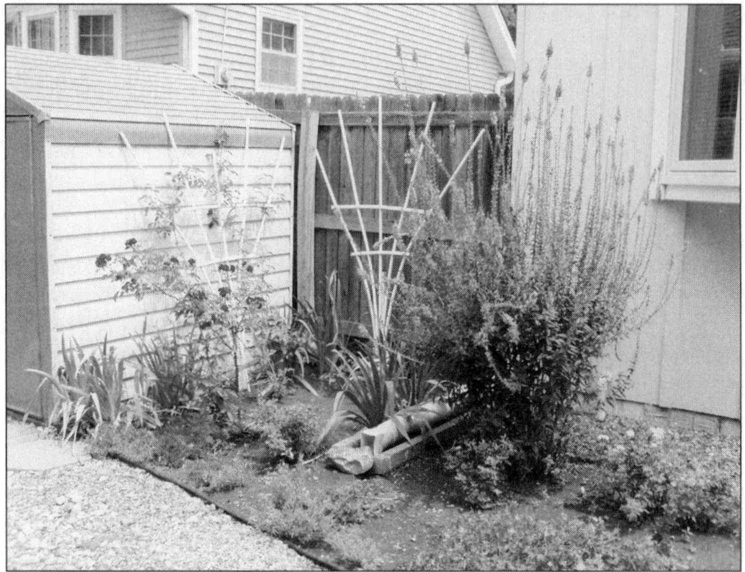

Photo courtesy of author

Figure 12-1: Spacing plants gives them room to grow and prevents clutter.

Trashing the trash

Make it easy to discard garden debris and yard waste. A compost bin at the back of the yard helps you recycle yard waste (see Chapter 7).

Keep a lidded garbage container for non-compostable waste in an easily accessible location — but remember to keep the location visually appealing and definitely out of the Wealth sector. (You don't want your garden looking like trash day every day.) An area screened by a lattice or some climbing plants works well. Figure 12-2 shows a well-hidden trash bin.

Photo courtesy of author

Figure 12-2: Can you spot it? The trash dumpster is hidden behind the squash vine.

Using Feng Shui Cures

For the best results, use Feng Shui cures intelligently, consciously, and with intention. In other words, don't just stick a bunch of crystals in a tree and hope for the best. Instead, understand what your Feng Shui problem is, select the best cure for the problem, set your intentions as you cure your problem, and *then* hope for the best.

Looking at the different cures

Certain areas of your garden may need some Feng Shui fixes to raise the chi and encourage the smooth and easy movement of chi throughout the space. The fixes, or *cures,* described in this section can help you keep chi moving, can slow down fast-moving chi or deflect negative chi, depending on your particular problem. Remember that fast-moving chi can happen in areas with lots of straight pathways; slow-moving or stagnant chi can happen in areas where the chi gets physically stuck and can't move around, and negative chi can happen when sharp angles project cutting (negative) chi toward you.

Light cures

Lighting raises the chi in an environment. And light is associated with the Fire element (and, therefore, the Fame sector), so it can be used to enhance Fire or Fame (or both).

The following list has a few lighting ideas for you to try out:

- Use outdoor lights, sconces, candles, and tiki torches to attract attention and lift energy. Also hang small Christmas tree lights in trees or wrap them around pillars.
- Hang outdoor chandeliers from a porch roof or pergola.
- Don't confine lighting to just the porch and deck area. Add path and walkway lighting throughout the garden, not just to guide your guests' feet but also to lift their spirits.
- Always replace burned out bulbs as soon as possible. Burned out bulbs represent used-up "dead" energy.

Upward lighting is more favorable than downward lighting. It casts fewer shadows and tends to add more flattering illumination to a space.

See Figure 12-3 for an example of a lighting cure.

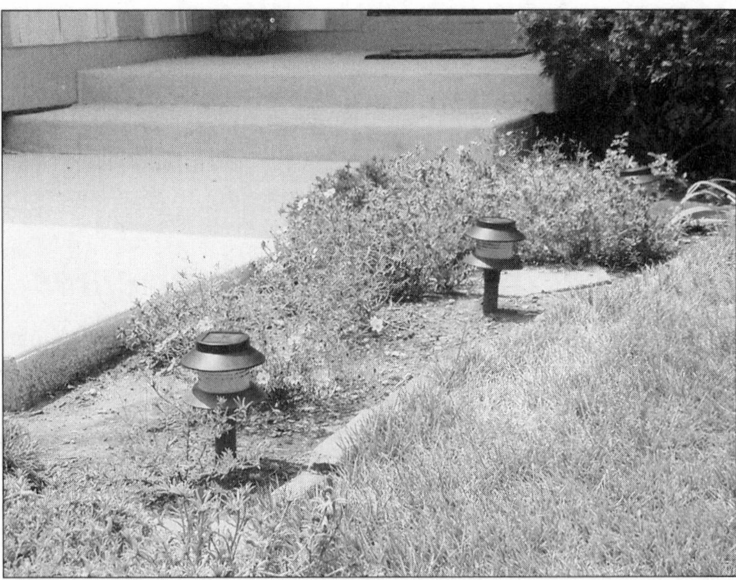

Photo courtesy of author

Figure 12-3: Lighting along paths raises chi.

Sound cures

Sound raises the chi and helps mask annoying noises (like the neighbor's motorcycle roaring up and down the street). Sound cures can be simple (placing a set of wind chimes on a tree branch) or complicated (adding an outdoor remote-controlled stereo system).

Wind chimes soften and dissipate sharp, negative energy. The sound symbolizes ringing in prosperity. So you can use them in the Wealth sector for a double dose of good Feng Shui!

Running water features — waterfalls and water fountains — also create a nice sound that raises the chi in your garden.

Color cures

Each of the Five Elements and each Life Sector of the Bagua has a color associated with it (for more on this topic, take a look at Chapter 3). Adding certain colors to your garden raises the chi. In general, the color red creates active, yang energy and can be used to raise the chi throughout the garden. See Chapters 3 and 7 for more information on using color in the garden.

Some colors create more active, yang chi and others less active, yin chi. In an environment where the chi is fast-moving and you already have lots of intense colors, you may want to create balance by adding yin colors. On the other hand, if you have an area of stagnant chi, you can add active yang energy to that area by adding yang colors. The following list helps you sort out which colors do what:

- Pastel colors have yin energy.
- Stronger, more vivid colors have yang energy.
- Red is the most yang of all colors.
- Orange is usually yang.
- Green, blue, and black are usually yin unless very bright.
- Yang colors create action.
- Yin colors relax people and make them feel more rested.

Don't forget that each of the life sectors has a special color associated with it. For example, the Fame sector is associated with the color red. To enhance the chi in a certain sector of the Bagua, use the color associated with that life sector.

Life energy cures

Living plants and animals create life energy that can raise the chi in your garden. So if a corner of the yard seems a little depressed energy-wise, let Fido loose — problem solved!

If you don't want to adopt a dog just to raise the chi, you can attract birds and other wildlife to your garden to help create more vibrant energy (see Chapter 11). See Figure 12-4.

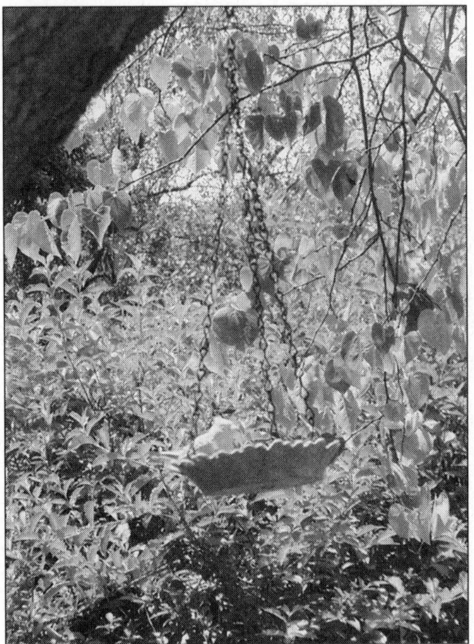

Photo courtesy of author

Figure 12-4: Attract birds with a feeder.

Kids = Life energy

Co-author Jennifer once lived on a block where you could never hear or see any children playing. It took her a year to figure out what was wrong and why the energy level in the whole place seemed depressed. Then she moved to a new neighborhood with a pile of kids running around, and right away she felt the place was much warmer and more welcoming!

Movement cures

You can help chi move throughout your garden by adding a movement cure — any object that moves, such as a weathervane, a flag, a pennant, or a whirligig (see Figure 12-5). These also attract attention and raise the energy level of guests.

Photo courtesy of author

Figure 12-5: This pinwheel makes a whimsical movement cure.

Stillness cures

Sometimes, too much living energy can create an abundance of yang energy, which makes it difficult to find peace and relaxation in your garden. Particularly in a contemplative spot, stillness cures work wonders.

Stillness cures are objects that don't move or grow. For example, you might place a few large boulders in a grassy area. That's it. The area is still and the boulders slow the chi down. The space is always quiet and ready for your deep, insightful thoughts.

Reflecting cures

You can deflect negative or cutting chi by reflecting it out of your garden. For instance, if a sharp corner on a building across the street directs an arrow of cutting chi at your garden, place an outdoor Bagua mirror above the entrance or on the fence to deflect that negative energy.

You can also use a Victorian gazing ball placed on a pedestal at or near an entrance to deflect negative energy back. The gazing ball can also be used in the garden itself to reflect the flowers and symbolically increase the abundance in your garden.

Crystals can be hung in trees to raise the chi in the garden. Remember to use real crystals, not the plastic imitators. Feng Shui can tell the difference! Quartz and amethyst are terrific chi activators.

Use glass or mirrored tabletops to enhance the chi in the garden, but make sure that they're in a safe place or that you can bring them in easily. You don't want them to get smashed in a hailstorm.

Guardian object cures

Add statues of animals, angels, spiritual items, or whatever is symbolically protective to you, to raise the chi in an area or to symbolically protect yourself from negative or cutting chi.

Traditionally, the Chinese used fu dog statues to symbolize protection.

Straight line cures

When the chi in an area seems stagnant and depressed, funnel more chi throughout the area by creating straight lines. Just add a straight walkway, plant a straight row of plants, or add a row of lights to the garden. See Figure 12-6.

Figure 12-6: This straight-line pathway keeps chi moving.

Curved line cures

When the chi moves too swiftly in an area (perhaps because of an abundance of straight lines), it leaves the environment too quickly to do much good.

To encourage chi to stay, add curved lines to the garden. A curving walkway, a series of plants set in a curved shape, and the like help to slow the chi down. You can add some bushy plants to a straight walkway in order to break it up a bit. See Figure 12-7.

© 2004 EDAW — photos by Dixi Carrillo

Figure 12-7: This curved line pathway keeps chi flowing smoothly.

Objets d'heart cures

Raise the chi in any part of your garden simply by adding something you love (what we call an "objet d'heart"). Maybe you're in love with that ceramic pot you found at a yard sale, or a plant that you spotted at the nursery last week, or an old cast-iron doorstop that your mother gave you. No matter what the object is, as long as you love it, it raises the chi in the garden. See a sample of an objet d'heart cure in Figure 12-8.

Photo courtesy of author

Figure 12-8: The gardener made this ceramic objet d'heart cure.

Combination cures

When you have a truly stubborn chi problem, you can try a combination of cures to fix it. Try one cure first, then another. For example, if a light cure doesn't do the trick entirely, add a color or sound cure.

Be sure to use compatible cures. If you need to raise the chi in a section of the garden, don't add both straight and curving lines expecting the combination to work. Instead, try a movement cure and a color cure.

Finding Mr. Right: The right cure, that is

With all the possible Feng Shui cures to choose from, how do you know which one is the right one for your pesky garden problem? Here's how to decide:

1. **Clear the clutter.**

   Cleaning up is always the first and best way to handle a Feng Shui problem.

2. **Fix the problem if you can.**

   If you have too much Metal, take some Metal away. Identify which area of the Bagua the challenge is occurring in and try to raise the chi by using an object or color associated with that life sector. For example, if the chi in your Wealth sector seems depressed, add the color purple or put in a Water element. See Chapter 6 for more information about raising the chi according to the characteristics of each life sector.

3. **If fixing the problem is not practical (for example, you're located next to a building that sends cutting chi your way, and you can't relocate), ask yourself if the problem is**

   Too much fast-moving yang energy?

   Too much slow-moving, stagnant yin energy?

   Negative, cutting chi?

   Then check out Table 12-1 to determine your next step.

4. **After consulting Table 12-1, start with a cure that appeals to you.**

   At the moment, we're very big on color cures, adding red to every place in the environment that needs livening up. One cure may appeal to you more than others; so start with that one first.

5. **If the cure you selected doesn't work (give it time), try another cure.**

   Cures can be used in combination with each other, so you don't have to replace a cure, you can supplement it with another cure. But make sure your use complementary cures, and don't let your cures create too much clutter in your environment, or you're interfering with the free flow of chi. If too much stuff piles up, remove an earlier cure.

6. **If all else fails, get in touch with a Feng Shui consultant.**

Table 12-1 Choosing the Right Cure for What Ails You

Problem	***Cures to Try***
Fast-moving yang energy	Slow it down using: • Stillness cures • Some color cures (yin colors slow down chi) • Curving line cures • Light cures to break the flow of or distract fast-moving chi • Sound cures (soft sounds for inviting chi to linger)

(continued)

Table 12-1 *(continued)*

Problem	*Cures to Try*
Slow-moving yin energy	Raise the chi using: • Light cures to liven and brighten the space • Sound cures to increase and activate chi levels • Some color cures (yang colors speed up chi) • Life energy cures • Movement cures • Straight lines cures • Objet d'heart cures
Negative, cutting chi	Deflect the chi and protect yourself using: • Reflecting cures • Guardian object cures

Setting intentions to cure Feng Shui problems

As you identify Feng Shui problems and try to solve them using cures, remember to always act with intention. Your *intention* is your stated goal for your action. If, for example, a corner of your garden has stagnant chi and you're planning to hang a wind chime to raise the chi, consciously say to yourself as you're hanging the wind chime that you're setting this cure with the intention of raising the chi in your garden, to make the garden a more friendly and welcoming place.

By stating what you want to do with the cure, you become clearer in your mind about what you want, and you pay more attention to creating a consciously designed garden.

Using intentions is necessary in all aspects of Feng Shui. If you want to enhance a Life Sector, you need to set your intentions while you're working in the Life Sector. You can say, "By planting these flowers, I bring abundance and prosperity into my life," or whatever your intention happens to be. Never underestimate the power of an intention!

Part IV
Thematically Speaking: Feng Shui and Theme Gardens

In this part . . .

If you want to follow a special theme as you create your garden, we've got you covered. In this part, we show you theme gardens with a twist — a Feng Shui twist. Whether you want to create a butterfly garden according to the principles of Feng Shui or you just want to grow some beets while welcoming abundance into your life, we show you how. Each chapter highlights a different type of theme garden and shows how to get started using the principles of Feng Shui.

Chapter 13

Aromatherapy-Herbal Garden

In This Chapter

- Growing herbs
- Picking plants
- Planning a Feng Shui garden design

Creating an aromatherapy-herbal garden is very Feng Shui! Not only can you use the herbs in your kitchen, but you can also use the smell to invigorate chi — a time-honored Feng Shui practice. (Think of burning incense.)

Combining the two makes good Feng Shui sense because good smells (the aromatherapy part) can raise the chi in any environment (and can perk you right up). Adding the herb part means you can use the garden in your kitchen, a very natural function that also creates good energy in your home. An aromatherapy-herbal garden can take up a very small space, so if you don't have a lot of room for a garden, this one can be ideal. You can still plant purple sage in your Wealth sector to bring abundance into your life even if you only have a windowsill on which to grow the garden.

Aromatic herbs increase the chi in the garden as they release their smell while growing; once harvested, you can use them personally to feel better, eat better, and raise your own spirits.

In this chapter, we describe how to choose the best plants for an aromatherapy-herbal garden, and how to plant such a garden the Feng Shui way.

Herbs 101

Herbs are used for food, medicine, and aromatherapy. Some herbs combine all three qualities, but most are used for only one main purpose and other uses are secondary.

Of the three main uses of herbs, we want to focus on two in this chapter: food and aromatherapy. Using medicinal herbs is extremely dangerous unless you know exactly what you're doing.

Although we talk about cooking herbs and aromatherapy herbs separately, the plants themselves can (and should) be combined into one garden because they complement each other. Also, some plants smell good and taste good.

Getting started

Grow herbs from seed or purchase them as starter plants. Some herbs actually do better when grown from seeds because they dislike being transplanted (basil, for instance). On the other hand, some herbs (sage, thyme) may not grow true from seed. Sigh. You can't win, can you?

A good resource is your local nursery or extension agency. They can also tell you which herbs grow best in local conditions, something you want to consider when you're choosing plants.

People used to find starter plants by picking wildflowers from parks and other public land (the side of the road). Be wary of using this method of collecting plants for your garden. Yes, these plants are free, but they could cost you: Some herbs are illegal to possess in some parts of the country and in some parts of the world. (Cannabis, anyone? Other herbs, too.) Also, strict laws protect endangered wildflowers, so before you pick those pretty flowers on the side of the road, make sure you're not breaking any laws.

Seeds are always cheaper than plants, so if cost is a concern, go with seeds. If you do choose to purchase plants, make sure you pick plants that look healthy — no brown spots, no wilting, no ugly holes from where the bugs have been chewing on them. Making sure that you bring only healthy plants into your garden keeps it healthy.

Hey, Herb, why grow herbs?

You can find plenty of reasons to grow herbs:

- They're user-friendly plants.
- They're beautiful.
- They're easy to grow.
- They don't require a lot of maintenance, care, or anxiety (already you feel better, right?).
- They're useful (they do more than look pretty).

For these reasons, creating an aromatherapy-herbal garden is a good choice for a beginning gardener. After you've built your confidence with an herb garden, you can move on to a veggie patch (a little harder) and then a full scale Feng Shui garden (a little harder than that).

If you're already an experienced gardener, an aromatherapy-herbal garden makes a nice addition to the flowers, trees, and shrubs you already know and love.

For ideas on different culinary, nonedible, and aromatic herbs to choose, see the section, "Picking Your Plants," later in this chapter.

Growing

Most herbs like full sun and light soil. Clayey soil doesn't work as well and should be amended before an herb garden is planted.

If soil quality is a problem, use a raised bed. A *raised bed* is a planter created by framing a section of land with wood or stones, then filling it with good quality soil — purchased from a nursery or garden center, not moved from the other side of the yard.

Occasional watering and weeding keeps your herb garden in tip-top shape. Don't overwater, but do keep the weeds under control, especially in a new garden, or they could choke out the herbs or stunt their growth.

Harvesting

When you create an herb garden, plan on continually harvesting the plants throughout the summer and early fall, as most of these plants produce for several months. In other words, you don't have just one harvesting season. (Well, if you harvest too much of the plant at once, you have only one harvesting season, 'cause you kill the plant. So if you use a lot of basil, grow a lot of basil plants.)

To get even more mileage from you herbs, you can bring some of the plants indoors for the winter so that you can continue growing sage for your stew even when you're snowed in. Now, that's convenient! If you do plan to bring any herbs inside for the winter, plant them in a pot first, and then plant the pot in the ground. You can easily dig up the pot come winter. This process isn't as traumatic for the plant as transplanting is.

When your herbs have reached maturity and are ready to be picked, follow these general guidelines for best results:

- Pick herbs on sunny days for peak flavor
- Use sharp scissors so as not to damage the plant
- Choose the best material to pick
- Harvest only a small quantity from any one plant
- Wipe picked plant material clean before drying

Preserving

You may want to preserve some herbs instead of using all the fresh plant material in your cooking. In fact, most gardeners plant more herbs than they can use during the growing season so that they can preserve the herbs and use them in the winter and early spring. You have many choices when preserving herbs. For example

- Herbs can be dried and crushed for use in cooking.
- Fresh or dried herbs can be preserved in vinegar or vegetable oil to add pizzazz to your salads and barbecues (Jennifer's personal favorite).

- You can create essential oils for aromatherapy use by distilling the essential oil of the plant (generally via steam distillation) and suspending it in vegetable or mineral oil.
- You can also preserve herbs in sugar, honey, and ice!

Picking Your Plants

When choosing plants for your aromatherapy-herbal garden, make sure that you end up with plants that create good chi energy — in other words, auspicious Feng Shui. See Chapter 3 for more information on chi.

This section provides tips and instruction for choosing various edible, nonedible, and aromatic herbs and alerts you to plants you should keep out of a Feng Shui garden.

Choosing culinary herbs

Using herbs you've grown yourself adds a special touch to even the most boring meal. A bit of oregano and basil from your garden makes even bland, canned pasta sauce worth eating.

Your herb garden should, for practical reasons, contain only herbs that are nontoxic unless you're an experienced herbalist. You wouldn't want to accidentally put a handful of toxic deadly nightshade leaves in your salad! (No, it's not nice to add them to your boss's salad, either.)

Make sure that you understand the characteristics and qualities of the herbs that you plant. Find out what they look like, how to tell when they're ready to be picked, and what part of the plant is used for cooking (sometimes it might be leaves, sometimes it might be seeds, and sometimes it might be roots.) See *Herb Gardening For Dummies,* by Karan Davis Cutler and Kathleen Fisher (Wiley Publishing, Inc.), for more information.

Choose herbs that you can use; don't pick a plant just because you need to have a yellow plant in the Relationship sector. Your personal preferences and what you like to cook should be your first consideration, and Feng Shui your next. See Chapter 6 for more information on the life sectors of the Bagua.

Check out the following list for common edible herbs for a beginner herb garden.

- Basil
- Bitter orange
- Black pepper
- Caraway
- Cardamom
- Chervil
- Chickweed
- Chicory
- Chives
- Cinnamon
- Coriander
- Cumin
- Dill
- Fennel
- French tarragon
- Garlic
- Garlic chives
- Ginger
- Horseradish
- Lemon
- Lemongrass
- Marjoram
- Mustard
- Onion
- Oregano
- Parsley
- Peppers
- Rosemary
- Sage
- Sunflower
- Thyme
- Turmeric

See Figure 13-1 for a late summer herb garden.

Choosing nonedible herbs

Nonedible herbs have many good uses. Read on and find out what they are.

Selecting safe medicinal herbs

Certain herbs are great to treat illnesses and to soothe cuts and scratches. However, unless you're knowledgeable and skilled in the art of using medicinal herbs, they should be avoided — particularly if they could be mixed up with the culinary herbs you plan to use in the kitchen.

See *Herbal Remedies For Dummies,* by Christopher Hobbs (Wiley), for further information about the medicinal uses of herbs.

Photo courtesy of author

Figure 13-1: This late-summer herb garden features purple sage.

A sensible precaution is to keep culinary herbs separate from medicinal herbs and to keep medicinal herbs clearly marked.

Insect repellant herbs

Some herbs have a smell that repels insects, so you may want to grow these for the purpose of keeping the bugs away:

- Wormwood dried in sachets repels moths
- Citronella essential oil if burned repels flying insects

For the cat

Don't forget catmint (catnip) if you have cats. The herb can be dried and stuffed in a felt toy to make your cat ecstatic.

Focusing on aromatherapy

While almost all herbs have a nice smell, not all of them are equally good choices for aromatherapy. And some plants that make wonderful aromatherapy material aren't what you normally think of as an herb. (Lemon springs to mind.)

A good aromatherapy plant has an attractive smell that can be used to stimulate or relax chi. (In other words, the smell can be used to perk you up or help you relax, depending on your needs.)

Usually, essential oils are extracted from the plant and the essential oils are used in aromatherapy. But sometimes, just sitting in a garden when the lavender is in bloom is all the aromatherapy you need!

Aromatherapy uses

Aromatic herbs can be effective as aromatherapy in several different ways:

- A few drops of essential oil in an essential oil burner give your spirits an immediate lift.
- A few drops of essential oil added to a potpourri or to a sachet create a nice scent in a room and help soothe tensions and relieve stress.
- Essential oils can also be added to the bath, for a relaxing indulgence.
- Properly diluted, essential oils can be used in massage oil for a real stress-relieving treat.
- In your garden, the scents that these growing plants give off can lift your spirits — just by sitting among them!

Using your nose: What good scents can do

Not all aromatic herbs (aromatherapy plants) affect your mood in the same way. If you need to perk up for a test you're about to take, you wouldn't want to rub chamomile massage oil on your shoulders. That'd put you to sleep!

See the following table for more information about what different scents are used for.

Scent	*Helps You . . .*
Basil	Counteract mental tiredness
Cardamom	Feel more energetic
Cedarwood	Calm down from shock
Chamomile	Fall asleep
Cinnamon	Focus
Citrus orange	Invigorate chi

Scent	***Helps You . . .***
Jasmine	Lift your spirits
Lavender	Relax and feel calm
Lemon	Stay calm and alert
Marjoram	Fall asleep
Peppermint	Stay awake and focus
Pine	Remain patient
Rosemary	Remain calm and attentive
Sandalwood	Feel less anxious

Avoiding certain plants

Plants that smell good create good energy in your garden, so how can you go wrong planting any plant that smells good? Well, you need to keep in mind a few other considerations. Plants with sharp spines (such as cacti) can create *sha* (cutting or negative) chi, and should be avoided, as should those that have pointed leaves, sharp edges, or thorns.

You can use them with care as long as there's no danger of the plants coming in contact with people. In general, though, choosing plants with rounded leaves and petals is better Feng Shui.

Creating a critter defense

In general, herbs don't suffer too many problems from pests or diseases. The strong smell keeps insects away, and because herbs are essentially wildflowers, they've developed tolerance of and resistance to pests and diseases.

But because insects don't like the smell, you can use certain herbs to protect other plants, like vegetables, from them! Plant the herbs in a row around the vulnerable plants to keep infestations down. This practice is called *companion planting.* For instance:

- Cotton, lavender, and curry discourage many insects.
- Chives and garlic repel aphids.
- Summer savory helps discourage blackfly.
- Marigolds repel whitefly (and rabbits).
- Chamomile is thought to improve the health of the plants around it.

Placing Your Plants with a Bagua

After you've selected the plants you want to put in your aromatherapy-herbal garden, you need to arrange them in the most auspicious way. To get the best results, use a *Bagua* (the eight-sided Feng Shui map that shows you how your physical environment corresponds with aspects of your life). See Chapter 6 for more on this handy-dandy Feng Shui tool.

To use the Bagua in an herb garden, simply apply the Bagua to a square or rectangular plot. Place the Career sector over the *entrance* (the direction from which you regularly approach) to your aromatherapy-herbal garden. If you don't have a main entrance to the plot, then place the Career sector so that it faces south. See Chapter 3 for more information on placing the Bagua.

Then, choose the locations for your plants by taking the characteristics of each Life Sector into consideration. If you want to enhance the chi in your T'ai Chi sector (the sector pertaining to overall health and wellness), plant something yellow there, such as yellow marigolds, because yellow is the color associated with that sector. If you want to enhance the chi in your Fame sector, plant something red there, such as a red pepper plant, because red is associated with the Fame sector. Because the Wood element is associated with the Family and the Wealth sectors, any plant placed there enhances the chi. You can further raise the chi by planting a green plant, such as basil, in the Family sector because green is associated with that sector and a purple plant, such as purple sage, in the Wealth sector because purple is associated with that sector.

Look at the Bagua in Chapter 3 and use your imagination:

- Considering that purple is the color associated with the Wealth sector, why not plant lavender in the southeast sector of the aromatherapy-herbal garden to see if it brings abundance to your life?
- A red plant, symbolizing the Fire element, can go in the Fame or south sector.
- A Water element can go in the Career sector, because Water is the element associated with that sector.

Use your own creativity to come up with ideas that suit your needs while following the principles of Feng Shui.

Chapter 14

Hummingbird Garden

In This Chapter

- Attracting hummingbirds
- Gardening for hummingbirds
- Keeping them safe

If you love the sight of hummingbirds hovering in space as they drink their fill of nectar, if you know they're the only birds that can fly backwards, and if you never mistake them for very large flying insects, then maybe you should consider creating a Feng Shui garden with a hummingbird theme.

Attracting hummingbirds brings vital living energy into your garden — which is an important part of Feng Shui. You can raise the chi in your garden just by getting a couple of ruby-throated hummingbirds to stop by and feed.

Creating a hummingbird garden doesn't have to be expensive or time-consuming. In fact, it's one of the easiest theme gardens to create. You can set aside a corner of your main garden for hummingbirds, or you can make it the focus of your entire backyard (although we gotta warn you that having a backyard full of hummingbirds creates a lot of yang energy and may spoil your plans to create a quiet contemplation corner).

In this chapter, we show you how to attract hummingbirds to your garden, feed them what they love to eat, and protect them from other animals that may mistake them for lunch.

Reading the Hummingbird Résumé

Hummingbirds are the smallest birds in the world and they have probably the highest metabolism. Most of their energy is spent in flying — up, down, forward, sideways, and backward. They beat their wings as much as 200 times per second. We're exhausted just thinking about it. Unlike your average bird (or plane, for that matter), they can stop in midair. Instead of a song, they have a chirping note. The buzzing sound you may hear when you're near a hummingbird is probably its wings! About 16 species of hummingbirds live in the United States and Canada. Not all hummingbirds migrate, but the ruby-throated hummingbird — the only hummingbird species found in the eastern U.S. — does.

This section tells you how to attract and care for these fascinating little creatures.

Attracting hummingbirds to your garden

Hummingbirds require vast stores of energy. Yep, they use up a ton of energy in order to eat a ton of food in order to get the ton of energy. . . .

Hummingbirds thrive on sugary fuel — the nectar they sip from the plants they visit. So they have to ingest lots and lots of food to survive.

Creating an outdoor aviary

When you create a space that attracts hummingbirds, you'll likely find that other birds — especially finches, orioles, and sparrows — like your garden, too.

In fact, you can create your own outdoor aviary where you can see all sorts of native birds without ever having to visit the zoo. See Chapter 11 for more information on encouraging all sorts of birds and other wildlife into your garden.

Don't forget that prime times for bird-watching are fall (as birds migrate for the winter) and spring (when birds return from migration for the summer).

Keep a journal listing the types of birds and the number of hummingbirds you see in your garden. As you make adjustments to your garden design, track the resulting changes in who visits your garden and when, and what they do when they're there.

Storing up fuel for flight

Before embarking on their fall migration, ruby-throated hummingbirds pack on an additional 50 percent of their normal bodyweight in fat to help them through their Gulf crossing. (Ruby-throated hummingbirds migrate to the Gulf of Mexico in the fall and return to North America in the spring.)

So what does a hummingbird look for in a garden? Consider the following:

- Red and other bright colors (orange, yellow, pink, and purple) are especially attractive to hummingbirds.
- Hummingbirds have long, slender bills to reach the nectar deep inside tubular flowers.

  Bees can't reach this nectar, which leads to the question: Which came first, the tubular flowers or the hummingbirds with their long slender bills? How did the tubular flowers spread their pollen before hummingbirds? How did hummingbirds survive without the nectar in tubular flowers? True hummingbird lovers care about these questions.

- Hummingbirds also eat insects, consuming as much as twice their body weight in food each day. That's a lot of grasshoppers. See Chapter 11 for more information on attracting insects to your garden to feed the hummingbirds.
- Hummingbirds like to take baths, but they prefer a light mist to a downpour (they may be small but they're not stupid). Use a misting device (available at larger pet stores and specialty bird stores) rather than a regular birdbath.

You can create a garden hummingbirds flock to in droves. (Or at least a few at a time.)

Giving your hummingbirds extra fuel

While you can plant specific flowers to attract hummingbirds (see the section "Planting for Hummingbirds" later in this chapter), you can also attract them by installing a hummingbird feeder filled with sugar water. (Think of sugar water as the hummingbird's version of chocolate.)

Use these feeders in the spring and fall to supplement the nectar that flowering plants produce because nectar is at a lower level at these times of year.

Hummingbirds remember a hummingbird feeder or group of nectar-rich plants from one year to the next.

Here are some tips to get the best results from hummingbird feeders:

- Pan-shaped and tubular feeders are both commonly used and equally effective.
- You can attract the attention of hummingbirds by tying a red ribbon near the feeder.
- Clean the feeder and replace the sugar water on a weekly basis, and do so more often in extremely hot weather. See the "Sugar water recipe" sidebar for a quick and easy recipe.
- Placing the feeder in the shade prevents most insects from using it. (Otherwise you might find more bees in your bonnet than hummingbirds in your garden.)
- Hummingbirds are territorial. If you want to reduce competition among the hummingbirds in your garden, hang several feeders throughout your garden. Keep them out of sight of each other for best results (sort of like small children in time out).

Sugar water recipe

Creating sugar water is easy. Just follow these simple steps:

1. Pour 2 cups of boiling water into a bowl or pitcher (be sure that the container is heat resistant).
2. Add ¼ cup of granulated sugar.
3. Stir together.
4. Cool the mixture.
5. Place mixture in hummingbird feeder.

This 8-to-1 solution is the best for hummingbirds; more sugar can be harmful to their health and less may not meet their energy needs. Don't use honey, which sometimes contains contaminants dangerous to hummingbirds.

Helping hummingbirds nest

Hummingbirds may create two (rarely three) nests a season because the females can produce eggs two or three times a season. Hummingbirds sometimes reuse a nest. Keep in mind that hummingbird nests are about half the size of a golf ball!

If you know what hummingbirds look for in a nest location, you may be able to provide it and enjoy the pleasure of watching a clutch of hummingbird eggs turn into hummingbird adults. Keep the following in mind:

- Hummingbirds generally pick deciduous (woody) shrubs and trees at least 3 yards off the ground — pines, poplar, dogwood, and oak trees are popular.
- Hummingbirds prefer nesting locations sheltered from the wind with dense foliage and a solid foundation.
- They frequently nest in the fork of a tree branch.
- They use thistle and dandelion down for the nest and attach it to the branches using pine resin and spider web. You can plant ferns, willow, and eucalyptus and encourage moss growth — hummingbirds use this plant material to make nests, too.
- You can also provide sterile nesting material for them, which is available at larger pet stores.
- Some companies also sell hummingbird houses for hummingbirds to use for nest building.
- Local birding groups (such as the Audubon Society) can provide relevant local information for your area. Your county extension agent may also have information on the nesting habits of the local hummingbird population.

Planting for Hummingbirds

In addition to placing hummingbird feeders at strategic locations throughout your garden, you can plant special flowerbeds designed to attract hummingbirds. Remember that tubular flowers in bright colors like red and orange are most attractive to hummingbirds, so think garish color palette rather than subdued hues.

Stay with native plants if you can. They're much more likely to survive and thrive under the climate conditions of your locale than an imported plant, no matter how pretty.

Plants that attract hummingbirds

Consider placing your hummingbird feeders in close proximity to your special hummingbird flowerbeds. The two sources of food reinforce each other, and your hummingbirds will remember that your garden is a fabulous source of food for a hungry avian.

See Table 14-1 for a list of plants that hummingbirds like, and the times of year in which they blossom.

Table 14-1 Plants That Attract Hummingbirds

Plant	***Season***
Bee balm	Summer/fall
Bluebell	Spring
Columbine	Spring/summer
Copper tip iris	Spring
Daylily	Summer
Fire bush (hummingbird bush)	Summer
Flowering quince	Spring
Flowering tobacco	Summer/fall
Four o'clock	Summer
Fuchsia	Summer/fall
Honeysuckle	Spring/summer
Phlox	Summer
Summer lilac	Summer

Plant your hummingbird garden so that plants flower throughout the year. Choose some plants that flower in spring, summer, and fall.

Keeping Feng Shui principles in mind

Designing a garden that attracts hummingbirds is good Feng Shui. Not only are these little birds attractive and comical, but they're also a *living energy cure* (see Chapter 12 for more on Feng Shui cures) for any stagnant, slow-moving chi problems you may have in your garden!

You don't have to create an entire hummingbird garden to use the living energy of a hummingbird to lift the chi. Try hanging a hummingbird feeder in an area of the garden with depressed energy and see what turns up! Instant living energy cure, small investment of time and money.

Balancing yin and yang energy

Hummingbirds are the embodiment of yang energy (see Chapter 2) as they flit from flower to flower, moving at a breakneck pace. They can also catch the eye and lift the spirits of visitors.

Because hummingbirds are so strongly attracted to bright colors, which create active, yang energy, and because hummingbirds give off a lot of yang energy themselves, make sure your garden doesn't become out of balance with too much yang energy.

Try balancing the brightly colored plants that attract hummingbirds with more subdued colors of plants in other areas of the garden.

Balancing the Five Elements in the hummingbird garden

If, for example, you plant your entire garden in red flowers to attract lots of hummingbirds, the garden will seem out of balance, according to the principles of Feng Shui. The Fire element (symbolized by the color red) may overshadow all the other elements. A garden with an overabundance of Fire element may be too active, with too much yang energy, which makes it a hard place to relax in.

To prevent this from happening, create islands of hummingbird-friendly plants throughout your garden, adding in plants of other types and colors that hummingbirds will ignore, but which balance out the Fire element and yang energy.

To find out more about the Five Elements and how to keep them in balance, see Chapter 6.

Protecting your tiny friends

In general, hummingbirds don't have to worry much about predators. However, kestrels, magpies, and hawks have been known to attack adult hummingbirds, and blue jays may steal their eggs. Cats nab hummingbirds now and then, and some have fallen victim to snakes, toads, and frogs.

You can keep hummingbirds safe (or at least safer) from felines by hanging feeders on a pole in the garden. Cats can't take hummingbirds by surprise if they have to scramble up a pole first, and if they can't leap from a nearby branch, they're frustrated in their search for a hummingbird snack.

You may have a harder time discouraging predatory birds from snacking on your hummingbirds, but you might try installing moving objects to frighten them off.

Keeping your hummingbird garden away from any pond or water feature helps prevent frogs, toads, and snakes from making off with your hummingbird visitors.

The Bagua and the hummingbird garden

The Bagua (see Chapters 3 and 6) is always at work, even in a hummingbird garden. It makes sense to place the hummingbird garden (or at least a bed of hummingbird-friendly flowers) in the Fame sector of the Bagua, which is associated with the color red and the Fire element. In other words, the kind of energy created by all those red plants and all those happy hummingbirds would do your reputation a great deal of good.

You could also add hummingbird-friendly plants to the Wealth sector of your garden, especially if you plant more purple-hued plants there. This raises the chi in your Wealth sector, creating more abundance and prosperity for you.

The Knowledge sector might not be the best place for a hummingbird garden, as the type of yang energy it creates could disrupt contemplation and thought.

Chapter 15

Butterfly Garden

In This Chapter

- Choosing plants that butterflies like
- Creating a home for butterflies
- Balancing your butterfly garden

If you've ever spent a summer afternoon chasing down butterflies in your backyard or in the neighborhood park marveling at all the different varieties of butterflies in existence, then you're probably open to the idea of creating a haven for these winged beauties.

Nostalgia isn't the only or even the best reason to create a butterfly garden, though. You can enhance the chi in your garden by setting aside a portion of it for butterflies. The living energy they create raises the chi — and creates a visual treat. In other words, butterflies are good Feng Shui.

A butterfly garden is also ecologically sound (the PC police are going to be proud of you). Because butterfly habitats are rapidly disappearing — owing to land development, creating a butterfly garden gives the insects a place to go and helps prevent them from disappearing entirely.

Don't forget, however, that butterflies start out as caterpillars. Well, okay, they start out as eggs. But the point is, when they're caterpillars, they eat the leaves of plants and can cause considerable damage in your garden. So know what you're getting into before you get started!

Planting for Butterflies

To coax butterflies into your garden, choose flowers that butterflies love, make sure they have places to sun themselves, and supply plenty of water to drink.

Finding out about butterfly species and local plants they're attracted to makes a great family project.

If you can avoid it, don't use herbicides and pesticides because they may poison the butterflies that come to visit your garden. Wouldn't that be pretty pointless? See Chapter 7 on ways to garden naturally.

Plants that attract butterflies are also likely to attract wasps and bees. If you have allergies to these bugs, you may want to rethink the whole butterfly garden idea.

Thinking like a butterfly when planting your garden

Butterflies get a little picky about where they want to live. (They have *conditions.* If they were human, they'd sit down and have a talk with you about their needs.)

So plan your butterfly garden while taking their — ahem! — needs into consideration:

- Because butterflies need shelter to feed and lay eggs, making the butterfly garden a protected space helps attract butterflies to it.
    - A windbreak of shrubs or trees can serve as a back to the butterfly garden.
    - Planting tall plants at the back and on the sides of the garden can also protect the garden (and, ergo, the butterflies) from wind.
- Graduate the height of the plants so that the shortest are in front (no special reason for this except that it helps you see the butterflies better).
- Plant the flowers so that similar colors are grouped together.
- Because butterflies need liquid, you may want to create a small section with wet sand or mud (butterflies get some nutrients indirectly from wet sand or mud).
- Different butterflies in different stages of the life cycle want different plants. See the section below, "Morphing through the life cycle of a butterfly."
- Butterflies are most active in mid- and late summer, so make certain that you have plenty of nectar-rich plants blooming then.

Morphing through the life cycle of a butterfly

Butterflies don't start out as butterflies. See the sidebar "The metamorphosis of a butterfly" to find out what they start out as. And, of course, not all kinds of butterflies want the same things. The point is, different butterflies want different things at different stages in their lives. Sort of like a high-maintenance date.

Finding out what caterpillars love

Keep in mind that during the voracious caterpillar stage, butterflies-to-be require different foods from when they become full-fledged butterflies. The following list features plants that caterpillars are especially partial to.

- Birch
- Daisy
- Elm
- Hollyhock
- Lilac
- Milkweed
- Poplar
- Snapdragon
- Trees

The metamorphosis of a butterfly

While the caterpillar stage of the butterfly's life cycle can be frustrating for a gardener, allowing your kids to see the metamorphosis of the butterfly is a kick.

Butterflies have an amazing life cycle. They begin their lives as eggs. Depending on the species, they're laid singly or in clusters with a bunch of siblings. As the egg hatches, an itty-bitty caterpillar emerges and eats its shell. Then it starts eating the plant that it's sitting on. Then it moves to the next plant over. Then the next plant. And so on. It molts (crawls out of its skin) several times before becoming a *pupa* — an intermediate stage during which it encloses itself in a cocoon and makes some adjustments to its internal organs as it prepares to become a butterfly. Eventually, the cocoon breaks up, and the adult butterfly emerges and spreads its wings.

Choosing plants that butterflies flit to

Different species of adult butterflies are attracted to different kinds of plants because they have different tastes in nectar. Just like people. Some of us are chocolate people; some of us are French fry people. Some of us are chocolate-*and*-French-fry people. Here are some points to keep in mind:

- **Choosing and planting a variety of butterfly-friendly plants is like offering a buffet to butterflies.** Each species can find something it likes. Just think of your garden as the all-you-can-eat salad bar in the neighborhood.
- **Butterflies like wild flowers *and* cultivated plants, so consider planting both types.** Just remember that some wild flowers butterflies like may actually be considered noxious weeds by your neighbors, so pay attention.
- **Pick plants that flower at different times of the year, even different times of day.** This way, plants will always be flowering and attracting butterflies to your garden.
- **Group members of the same plant species together.** Butterflies have a harder time finding single flowers. (Notice how all the fast food joints cluster together just off the highway? Same principle.)

Your county extension agent can advise you on local plants that are likely to attract butterflies to your garden. The agent can also tell you where to find information on butterflies native to your area.

Here's our standard disclaimer: No two butterfly garden experts actually agree on which plants butterflies are most likely to be attracted to. So do your own research. Keep a journal and try different plants, noting which ones seem most successful in your area. Then work on contradicting anyone who says otherwise. In no time at all, you, too, will be a butterfly garden expert.

See Table 15-1 for plants that butterflies adore (probably, but don't quote us).

Table 15-1 Plants Popular with Various Butterflies

Butterfly	*Plant*
Black swallowtail	Butterfly weed, alfalfa
Checkered skipper	Aster
Checkered white	Bee balm

Butterfly	***Plant***
Monarch	Cosmos
Orange sulfur	Marigold, zinnia
Painted lady	Hyacinth, zinnia, many others
Two-tailed swallowtail	Geranium
Wood nymph	Clematis

See the following list for other plants treasured by many species of butterflies (at least sometimes in some locations as seen by some gardeners, but we make no promises):

- Azalea
- Black-eyed Susan
- Blueberry
- Butterfly bush
- Coneflower
- Daylily
- Goldenrod
- Hibiscus
- Impatiens
- Lavender
- Lilac
- Phlox

Figure 15-1 is proof that butterflies like coneflowers. Notice how a caterpillar has destroyed the leaves of the coneflower. Nobody's perfect.

If you're looking for user-friendly plants to populate your butterfly garden — you want the butterflies but not the gardening — check out the following list for suggestions:

- Coneflower
- Cosmos
- Dill
- Parsley

- Verbena
- Zinnia

These plants are hard to kill. You have to *try.*

Many herbs are attractive to butterflies, so you can create an aromatherapy-herbal garden (see Chapter 13) that doubles as a butterfly garden! The following herbs are especially attractive to various types of butterflies:

- Anise
- Catnip
- Chives
- Dill
- Parsley
- Peppermint
- Rosemary
- Spearmint
- Sweet Fennel
- Thyme

Photo courtesy of author

Figure 15-1: Butterfly snacking on coneflower.

Also, many plants that attract hummingbirds (see Chapter 14) also attract butterflies. So you can have a garden alive with both hummingbirds and butterflies — imagine how much yang energy that'll create! However, do be aware that the hummingbirds may eat the butterflies. If you still want to attract both, try

- Daylily
- Flowering tobacco
- Four o'clock
- Lupine

Coaxing Butterflies to Visit

Besides planting flowers that butterflies like, you can make your garden attractive to butterflies by providing them with supplemental food and places to bask in the sun.

Providing supplemental nectar

You can make butterfly feeders to supplement the nectar produced by the flowers in your garden. These feeders make a quick and fun project with the kids. Just expect to end up with sticky hands and countertops.

Making a jar feeder

To create a jar feeder, you need

- A small jar, such as baby food jar, with lid
- A wad of cotton
- Sugar-water solution (see below)
- Brightly colored string or ribbon, about 18 inches

  Red string is used a lot in Feng Shui — the length of which is always in multiples of nine (a very auspicious number).

- Drill

After you gather your supplies, follow these simple steps:

1. **Drill a small hole in the lid of the jar.**
2. **Feed a piece of cotton through the hole.**
3. **Fill the jar with sugar-water solution.**

   See the "Sugar-water solution" sidebar.

Sugar-water solution

Making a sugar-water solution for butterflies is easy. Just follow these easy steps:

1. Mix one part of sugar with nine parts of water. (For the mathematically challenged, one teaspoon of sugar combined with nine teaspoons of water or one cup of sugar combined with nine cups of water. But you'd never use up nine cups of sugar-water solution in a year, so go with the teaspoons. Or tablespoons.)
2. Boil the sugar and water together for several minutes until the sugar dissolves.
3. Cool and pour into your butterfly feeder.

4. **Attach the lid to the jar.**
5. **Tie the string around the jar.**
6. **If needed, glue the string to the jar.**
7. **Hang the jar in a tree near but slightly above nectar-producing flowers.**

Clean the feeder and change the sugar water and cotton every week, more often in extreme heat.

Making a dish feeder

For the mechanically challenged, an even simpler feeder:

1. **Select a flat dish.**
2. **Place a wad of cotton or tissue on it.**
3. **Glue a string to the dish so that it can be hung from a tree near nectar-producing flowers.**
4. **Add the sugar-water solution (see the sidebar, "Sugar-water solution").**
5. **Hang the feeder from a tree.**

Make sure to clean the dish and change the solution at least once a week (more frequently in hot weather).

Knowing why butterflies stay

What do butterflies look for in a home? In addition to plants that provide them food when they're caterpillars and with nectar when they're butterflies, butterflies also want

If all else fails, buy the darn things!

If you're having trouble attracting butterflies to your garden, or want to supplement the butterflies that do show up, you can purchase butterflies from garden supply stores. Remember to choose species native to your region so they have a good chance of surviving and thriving in their new home.

- Plenty of direct sun during the day (butterflies are insects, so they need the sun to regulate their internal temperatures)
- Plants where they can lay eggs
- Places to hibernate
- Flat rocks for basking

Butterfly houses — similar to birdhouses but with slots just the size to let butterflies in and keep birds out — may also encourage butterflies to visit your garden. Purchase them at larger nurseries and garden supply stores.

Balancing Living Energy with Still Energy

Don't forget that the principles of Feng Shui are in full force in a butterfly garden. Consider that having a garden full of butterflies might someday seem like a hive full of bees. In other words, they create lots of yang energy as they flit from flower to flower. To counteract all that craziness, consider the following:

- Instead of creating an entire garden for attracting butterflies, consider planting just one raised bed.
- Alternate butterfly-attracting plants with those that don't attract butterflies.
- Remember to keep a balance between living energy and still energy — yang and yin. So if you have lots of butterflies in your garden, balance that energy with open areas of calm yin energy — perhaps a tranquil water feature and dark-colored plants or structures.

And don't forget to place a bench or chair nearby for you to sit and enjoy your handiwork!

Chapter 16

Zen Garden

In This Chapter

- Defining the Zen garden
- Choosing a quiet spot
- Creating your Zen garden
- Picking some great objects
- Keeping chi moving

Does a peaceful garden spot where you can quietly sip a cup of tea sound like your cup of tea? Does creating a haven from the stresses of the day, a place where you can actually think about Life with a capital "L" sound like the cure to your busy, over-scheduled life (with a lowercase "l")? Maybe you'd just like to read the morning paper without being interrupted.

If so, you may want to think about creating a Zen garden. Zen gardens, originally created by Zen Buddhist priests as an aid to meditation, are Japanese in origin, unlike Feng Shui, which comes to us from the ancient Chinese. Even so, a Japanese Zen garden can be adapted to provide a perfect Feng Shui design.

In fact, you'd have a hard time creating a Zen garden with bad Feng Shui, although someone somewhere has probably managed it. But it won't be you, because you have us.

In this chapter, we explain just what a Zen garden is and go over some practical reasons why you may want to create a Zen garden of your own. And we show you how to create one according to the principles of Feng Shui. We also clue you in on how to keep the chi moving in such a low-key place.

What's a Zen Garden?

Before you can decide whether you want to create a Zen garden, you need to know what one is (makes sense, right?). Zen priests call these gardens *kansho-niwa* or *contemplation gardens:* The entire garden is intended to help create a deeper understanding of Zen Buddhist concepts.

However, the term "Zen garden" is often applied to any type of dry-landscape-style Japanese garden. In other words, you can adapt Zen-style gardens to your own interests and needs. You don't have to use your Zen garden to dwell on Zen concepts (although you can). Most people enjoy their Zen gardens as havens from stress and pressure. Visiting your Zen garden can be like going on a retreat, without all that annoying packing.

The main virtue of the Zen garden is its simplicity. This simplicity actually makes the garden more flexible than you may think. A Zen garden can be almost anything you want it to be, as long as you keep it simple. For example, sand and stone make up the typical Zen garden. You could add one or two bright plants in dramatic containers. That'd be okay. But if you start adding ten plants and vines climbing up trellises and lots of lawn furniture, you're getting away from the concept of Zen gardening.

Why Zen?

Sure, sure, you want some peace and quiet. Who doesn't? But you can get that by locking yourself in the bathroom. What else is in it for you if you go the Zen garden route? The following list provides just a few of the reasons a Zen garden may be desirable:

- **Water conservation:** Because Zen gardens require relatively few plants, they're a good choice in areas undergoing drought or in arid and semi-arid regions. People concerned about water conservation can still get enjoyment out of their gardens while sticking to their principles.
- **Minimal maintenance:** A garden with few plants has minimal maintenance requirements, making it a fine choice for people without a lot of time or patience for gardening. If you take care of other people or places all day long and would like your garden to take care of you, the Zen garden is your best bet.
- **Fits anywhere:** You don't need much room to create a Zen garden, so you can choose a small part of a larger garden; or, if you have only a small space, you can create a Zen garden to take advantage of that space. You can put a Zen garden on a rooftop or on a small patio. (See Chapter 19 for more about gardening in small spaces.)

The idea is that instead of overwhelming the senses, you protect them, allowing yourself the chance to really see what's in front of you, for the purpose of seeing what's inside you. (That almost sounds profound.)

Designing with Tranquility in Mind

Because Zen gardens are supposed to be places to rest and meditate, you want your space to be as simple and peaceful as possible. Achieving tranquility isn't difficult, but it does require some thought and planning. In this section, we discuss what you need to do to create a tranquil Zen garden.

Planning your garden

As we've said before, the purpose of a Zen garden is to create feelings of tranquility and calm. Keep this function in mind as you plan. Getting frustrated enough to tear your hair out while you're trying to find the perfect place for that priceless boulder from Colorado defeats the purpose of creating a Zen garden. Even the construction of a Zen garden should be pleasant and enjoyable. If you're getting frustrated and angry while you build yours, re-think what you're doing.

The basic rule of Zen gardening, as we keep repeating, is to keep it simple, simple, simple. So keep the following ideas in mind as you plan your garden:

- **Start with the bare minimum and slowly add additional pieces to the garden.** For example, start with one or two stones, then add a plant. Later, add a decorative object if you decide that it's necessary.
- **Avoid complicated garden designs.** If you're a real plant lover, you may be tempted to plant beds of your favorite annuals in your Zen garden because they're so pretty. But getting complicated sort of defeats the whole purpose of creating a Zen garden. A single plant or a container holding several plants is fine. An entire flowerbed — not so much.
- **Keep the garden empty and still so it's a place where you can recharge your batteries.** Remember that the idea is to provide relief from the stresses and pressures of everyday life.
- **Find one perfect object to focus on — whether it's a plant or a stone or a statue.** Finding this one perfect object is more important than acquiring lots of goodies for your garden. See Figure 16-1 for an example of what we mean.

Figure 16-1: This striking cobalt blue vase against stone steps is very Zen.

Contemplating the location

You probably don't want to turn your entire backyard into a Zen garden, although you can. (We won't stop you. Heck, we may come visit.) If you *do* turn your entire backyard into a Zen garden, you may want to place an appropriate object, plant, or tree in each sector of the Bagua to enhance the chi in that sector. But be careful about overdoing it and use plants and objects that are thematically related to each other.

You're probably going to choose a corner of your yard to turn into a contemplative retreat, especially if you have to share your yard with others (kids, dogs, the landlord). But which corner of your yard should you choose?

Because contemplation is generally attempted in private, you should choose the backyard for the Zen garden — the front and side yards are more public environments. So where in the backyard should your Zen garden go?

In most cases, the best place for the garden is in the Knowledge sector (see Chapter 6).

You can also place the Zen garden in the center of your garden, the T'ai Chi sector, because that's the area of overall health and well-being. However, if you place the Zen garden in the center of your yard, you may be distracted by the other functions going on in your yard, such as the kids playing catch in the Children sector.

Because the energy in a Zen garden is very yin and passive, and the purpose of the garden is to allow you time for thought and reflection, avoid placing the Zen garden in Life Sectors where you would benefit more from yang energy and elevated chi.

Don't place the Zen garden in the Fame sector, for example, because you may get interrupted repeatedly because the Fame sector has to do with people (what they think about you mostly, but people), so the Fame sector attracts visitors. And if you put a place for solitary contemplation in the Relationships sector, you may find that you're doing more than your contemplation solo.

Keeping out noise and activity

Because your Zen garden should be restful, you want to divert noise and activity that disrupts the calm and tranquil energy of the place. Keep the play area away from the Zen garden. You don't want Rover digging in the sand or Fluffy using it as an outdoor litter box. Tucking the garden around a corner and surrounding it with hedges or a fence may help reduce the amount of noise and activity that intrudes.

Try to position the Zen garden so it's not directly in the path of an entrance to the house or main yard. This reduces the traffic flow in the area.

Because you're using fewer plants, you have fewer wildlife visitors, which keeps the operation low-key.

You can choose to use the Zen garden at times of day when you're least likely to be disturbed. Make that part of your planning. If you expect to use the Zen garden at lunchtime, then take into consideration that the sun is high in the sky at that time of day and you may want to factor in some shade.

Sand and Stone: The Essence of Zen Gardening

A traditional Zen garden has two main parts: sand and stone. The stones or rocks symbolize mountains and the sand symbolizes flowing water. Yes, you could actually get water itself to symbolize water, but that would not be as cool.

One great feature of Zen gardens you may not be familiar with is "playing with the sand" to create relaxation. You're not supposed to think of this as a chore, like raking leaves. Rather, it's a sort of physical meditation that allows you to free your mind to contemplate infinity, or something like that. A rake with wide-spaced tines is used to move the sand around and to create straight, wavy, or circular patterns. If raking the sand persists in seeming like a chore to you, put the rake down until you've achieved a higher level of enlightenment.

The sand traditionally used in Japanese Zen gardens is not beach sand or play sand. It's actually crushed granite. (Granite is better suited to raking.) Ask at your local garden supply store, and check online as some mail-order garden supply stores carry the appropriate sand.

Making the sand-and-stone garden

Usually, a rectangular site is chosen for the sand-and-stone garden and laid out on a flat, clear space of ground. This part of the garden can be any size you want, but do try to keep it in proportion with the overall yard. The site you choose should be protected from high winds (or else you get to see firsthand what a sandstorm looks like). Choose the location carefully for the most tranquil view and setting. Then:

To make your sand-and-stone garden, gather the following materials:

- Framing materials, either timbers or concrete blocks, bricks, stones or tiles
- Fabric liner
- Sand or crushed granite
- Rocks or boulders
- Bench

1. **Build a frame.**

   Nail timbers together and partially bury them to make a frame for the sand and stones. Concrete blocks, bricks, stones, or tiles can also be used to keep the sand from blowing away. They can be laid on top of each other. The first layer should be partially buried for stability.

2. **Remove any grass and plantings from the interior of the frame.**

3. **Place a fabric liner on the ground to prevent weeds from growing up through the sand in the garden.**

4. **Place sand on top of the liner to a depth of several inches.**

5. **Arrange a few rocks in aesthetically pleasing designs.**

   See the section, "Choosing the rocks," for more on this essential task.

6. **Place a low wooden bench near the stone-and-sand garden.**

Choosing the rocks

In Japanese Zen gardening, the rocks are generally chosen for their resemblance to natural objects, and these natural objects in turn symbolize a prized quality. For example, the tortoise and the crane represent longevity, so rocks that symbolize the tortoise and the crane are often used in the garden. We recommend that you don't select rocks shaped, for instance, like a toilet.

When choosing rocks for your garden, keep the following tips in mind:

- Choose large stones in a variety of shapes and sizes. You only need a few.
- The stones you pick should be well weathered and have some character.
- If their shapes symbolize something meaningful, so much the better. Pick shapes that have personal resonance for you.
- Remember to keep the size of the stones in proportion with the rest of the garden. An overwhelming boulder in a tiny sand-and-stone garden may seem subtly or energetically threatening compared to a slightly more scaled down version.
- Place the stones in the sand and stone garden in a way that pleases your eye.

Creating the Zen Landscape with Simple Objects

Your Zen garden doesn't have to consist only of sand and stone. In fact, it doesn't have to consist of sand and stone at all, although in that case, you may call it a Japanese-style garden or dry landscape garden rather than a Zen garden.

The idea is to keep the space relatively empty and to add in only a few objects of simple design and great visual and emotional appeal. See Figure 16-2 for an example of a new twist on the ancient art of Zen gardening.

© 2004 EDAW — photography by Dixi Carrillo

Figure 16-2: A modern interpretation of a Zen garden.

Try your own twist. For example

- Instead of using sand, create an open grassy space with a few boulders or stones that appeal to you. (***Hint:*** We're not going for Stonehenge here.)

- Pave a space with beautiful tiles and add one or two statues that you find particularly appealing.
- Put down white rock pebbles and add a few pieces of driftwood and a low cedar bench.

Always consider the impact of adding additional objects before doing so. Don't be afraid to take things *out* of your Zen garden. Think simple visual appeal.

Bridges can be used to link areas of your Zen garden together and to bring guests into your Zen garden from the larger world. These bridges can be kept natural or painted to bring a little yang energy into the garden.

Using native plants to create a Zen garden

Although you can use traditional Japanese plants in your Zen garden — for example, a cherry blossom tree — using plants native to your locale gives an unexpected twist to your garden. And local plants are likelier to survive and thrive in local conditions.

When picking your plants, remember

- Only a few plants are needed. Pick plants of different shapes, sizes, and colors.
- In Feng Shui, an odd number is thought to be more auspicious than an even number of plants.
- Choose your very favorites, and be ruthless about selecting only a few and only the best.
- Before planting them in the ground, consider placing them in pots and setting the pots around your Zen garden. This means you can contemplate the arrangement of your plants and find the most appealing positions before making the planting final.
- Also, the pots themselves can add some visual impact to the garden if you select them with an eye toward their aesthetic punch.

Choosing other local objects

Be sure to choose rocks and other objects native to your area. Go to the local quarry and handpick a few of the most interesting ones. Get in touch with local landscapers and offer to take any rocks they dig up off their hands. Using local rocks keeps your Zen garden in tune with your local environment, which is good Feng Shui.

Choose a local alternative to crushed granite sand. Maybe you can use river rock or gravel in your Zen garden.

Pick decorative objects created by local craftspeople using local materials. Or, if you have a creative bent, make them yourself!

Keeping Your Zen Garden Feng Shui-Friendly

A Zen garden can have good Feng Shui because creating a Zen garden is about choosing objects with care and placing them with thought and intention. However, because Zen gardens have certain characteristics (for example, lots of wide open spaces), Feng Shui problems can creep up on you. But we've got a handle on them, and so can you.

Preventing stagnant chi

Because a Zen garden is quiet and empty, chi can sometimes become stagnant and get stuck. That makes your Zen garden depressing rather than relaxing. Uh-oh. To avoid that problem, make sure the chi can move freely throughout the space. Here are a few suggestions:

- Plant a few more plants — perhaps colorful blossoming flowers. You don't need to add many, just a few carefully chosen ones selected for their appeal and for their dramatic potential.
- Install some lighting in the garden in the form of tiki torches, candles, or outdoor fixtures. Again, be sure to choose a lighting source that has interesting visual appeal.
- Hang some soft-sounding bamboo wind chimes. They raise the chi while maintaining the tranquility of the space.
- Although traditional Zen gardens don't have water features, adding one to yours can help move the chi throughout the space. Place the water feature in the center of the garden as an object of contemplation. The gentle sound of running or rippling water is relaxing to many people. See Figure 16-3 for an example of a simple fountain that looks good in a Zen garden.

Figure 16-3: A simple water feature can keep chi moving in a Zen garden.

Letting the chi enter your garden

Make sure that chi can get *into* your Zen garden in the first place. You may want to block out noise and activity, but don't block out the chi. Make sure it can enter the garden through a gate or openwork fence.

To keep chi moving, give it a path to follow. You can create a simple path through your Zen garden that allows you, your guests, and the chi to move from one part of the garden to another.

Achieving balance and harmony

A Zen garden is all about finding balance and harmony — and that's what Feng Shui is about, too. But the Feng Shui principles, such as the Five Elements, can get out of whack in a Zen garden because the Zen garden has so few items and objects in it.

Balancing yin energy with yang energy

The Zen garden contains mostly yin energy, which is good because you use this spot to meditate and contemplate. However, if the yin energy becomes *too* dominant, you may need to inject a bit of yang energy to prevent your garden from becoming a depressing place to be. Perhaps the yang energy could come from an object, such as a plant pot, painted in a bright color. Keep in mind that rocks are considered yang energy, so you may simply need to add a few more large rocks to the garden to bring it into balance.

Balancing your Zen garden with the rest of your yard

You also want to balance the Zen garden space with the larger yard beyond it. Make certain that a transition exists between the Zen garden and the rest of your yard, and that the rest of your yard has yang energy to balance the yin energy of the Zen garden.

A possible way to do this is to place a lattice screen or archway as a transition, or you can plant a hedge. Or create a living segue from one part to another by gradually adding more plants and objects as you leave the Zen garden.

Chapter 17

Taoist Garden

In This Chapter

- Defining the Taoist garden
- Deciding what you need
- Creating a Taoist garden

If you think Mother Nature paints a better picture than Picasso, the Taoist garden may just be for you. Traditional Chinese gardens, sometimes called *Taoist gardens,* are based on the Taoist belief that nature is the superior art form and that we should take our artistic and creative cues from the natural world. Thus, Taoist gardens are tranquil yet dramatic, just like the natural world.

Nature is the starting point in a Taoist garden, but the underlying secret is that nature can always be improved upon — or at least helped out a bit. The goal is to create a garden that looks natural, not man-made. Of course, that doesn't mean that you can sow some wildflowers and sit back. A Taoist garden creates a different beautiful scene in each season, because nature itself is beautiful in each season — even when you're freezing your mustache off. The back-to-nature approach of Taoist gardening is, of course, very Feng Shui. (See Chapter 2 for more on the basic principles of Feng Shui.)

In this chapter, we show you how to make a Taoist garden that'll impress even Mother Nature, using timeless Feng Shui principles and techniques. An important principle of Taoism is connecting with nature and making nature more beautiful; an important principle of Feng Shui is to place the objects in the best place for them. A Taoist garden created according to Feng Shui principles is one in which the beautiful objects of nature are placed in the most favorable places for them.

Understanding What a Taoist Garden Is

Taoist gardens, which are usually created as contemplative settings, look natural, even if great effort goes into their care. They're meant to look as if they'd just accidentally grown that way, but they're actually carefully planned (sort of like co-author Jennifer's naturally auburn curls that require a slight assist from the local beauty salon).

Taoists gardens also have an aspect of theater about them — they're designed for maximum impact (again like Jennifer's auburn curls). This impact can only be achieved through careful planning and the selection of the right plants and decorative objects for your garden. For instance, in a typical garden, you may plant masses of flowers in a bed and be pleased with the overall impact of the flowerbed (Jennifer's preferred approach). In a Taoist garden, however, you carefully choose one flower or plant, and place it against a wall or other backdrop for dramatic visual effect.

If you're a person to whom dramatic elegance appeals, a Taoist garden may be just right for you. In other words, if people use words like "exotic" and "unusual" to describe your home rather than "comfy" and "country," you probably have a flair for Taoist designs. A Taoist garden uses the natural world in new and eye-opening ways, framing natural objects in unexpected ways and highlighting the most beautiful examples of nature.

Looking at the Pieces of a Taoist Garden

Taoist gardens include natural objects from three main categories: stones, water, and trees. The use of these objects is balanced with open spaces. Finally, the element of surprise is an essential part of a Taoist garden.

Stones, water, and trees

The Taoist garden includes three crucial categories of objects:

- **Stones and boulders:** As in a Zen garden (see Chapter 16), stones symbolize mountains in the Taoist garden.

  Large stones are chosen for their patterns and shapes. Small stones are set into walls or hung on them, as objects of contemplation. All rocks are chosen for their character and symbolism — the more moss and lichen, the better. For good symbolism, choose rocks in the shapes of favorable Chinese animal symbols, such as turtles, dragons, and fish.

Some Taoist gardens include huge boulders big enough to walk through, but you don't have to put these in your garden unless you want to.

Name your rocks. Consciously choose the rocks and stones you want to place in your landscape and think about what they represent to you. There's nothing wrong with having Crouching Tiger and Hidden Dragon just on the other side of the compost bin!

- **Water features:** Water features (the more natural appearing, the better) bring chi into the garden, and reflect the sky and landscape, symbolically enlarging the garden. And water symbolizes wealth and abundance; so placing the water feature of your Taoist garden in the Wealth sector (see Chapter 6) is good Feng Shui!

  Moving water brings sound into the garden, which also helps raise the chi.

  Water features, such as ponds, often have an island in the middle to symbolize the dwelling place of the ancient Immortals, the revered ancestors of the ancient Chinese. Trees are not planted on islands. See the section, "Creating a Rockery," for more information on putting a water feature into your Taoist garden.

- **Trees:** Trees (and other plants) are chosen for their permanence and are thought to develop a relationship with their environment over time. Thus, the plants are selected with great care, because replacing them every year isn't an option.

In Taoist gardens, the color of the trees and plants is not an important consideration, although in Feng Shui design, it is. Because you're designing this Taoist garden to adhere to Feng Shui principles, you probably want to choose plants with some consideration of color and how they fit into the balance of the Five Elements and the Life Sectors of the Bagua (see Chapter 6 for further information).

Open spaces

The three categories of objects — stones, water, and trees — are balanced with open spaces in the Taoist garden. The amount of open space should be in proportion to the other objects in the garden. Huge acres of wide-open prairie dotted with a couple of small stones won't do the job. Open areas should be used as breathing room between artistically arranged objects and plantings.

Think of these open spaces as paths between one area of impact and another.

Bridges and pathways

Bridges and pathways connect various parts of the garden. You can use these bridges and pathways to move the chi throughout the garden; for good Feng Shui, they should curve, allowing the free flow of chi throughout the garden. Straight paths may cause the chi to move too swiftly through the garden.

Bridges and walkways can be designed to showcase the garden from different views as well. Often, Taoist gardens have walkways that zigzag throughout the garden, taking unexpected turns and detours to show the garden from all angles. As long as these paths don't funnel chi too quickly through the garden, and as long as sharp angles and corners are softened with plantings to avoid the creation of cutting (negative) chi, such zigzag paths are well in keeping with Feng Shui principles.

See Figure 17-1 for an example.

Elements of surprise

The Taoist garden usually has something up its sleeve. You turn a corner and suddenly face an interesting statue. You step through an archway and into a garden bursting with color. In a Taoist garden, the gardener uses decorative objects to make surprising, bold statements about himself.

Now and then, add something new to the garden in order to keep the surprises fresh. Here are a few ideas:

- At holiday time, add a potted pine tree festooned with twinkling lights.
- At harvest, create a tableau of autumn delights — decorative corn and gourds, pumpkins, a bale of hay.
- Add a papier-mâché dragon or a string of Chinese lanterns for the Chinese New Year (which is in late January or early February, depending on the year).

Amusing surprises are an important part of the Taoist garden. See Figure 17-2 for a garden nook that showcases a few surprises.

© 2004 EDAW — photography by Dixi Carrillo

Figure 17-1: This walkway leads visitors on a zigzag course through the garden.

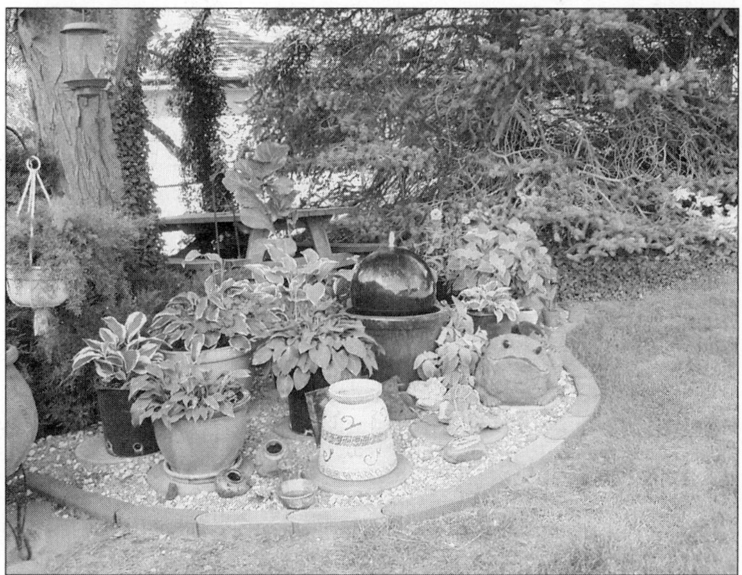

Photo courtesy of author

Figure 17-2: This garden serves up some smiles!

Planning and Creating Your Own Taoist Garden

You've got a fine sense of the theatrical, and you've got a green thumb. Now you just need to put the two together to create a Taoist garden — the Feng Shui way, of course.

Choosing, planting, and caring for plants

Creating a Taoist garden requires choosing appropriate plants for the space. Be picky, picky, picky. In a typical garden, many problems can be overlooked as long as you have a bunch of pretty plants in a bunch of pretty colors bunched together. In a Taoist garden, however, each plant deserves its own spot with its own attention. Each plant has space around it so that it can be appreciated for itself. Some points to keep in mind:

- As we mentioned earlier, trees are extremely important in the Taoist garden. Invest most of your time and money in choosing the right trees for your garden (what makes it right is up to you).

  One or two trees balanced with a selection of rocks and a water feature may be all you need to get started.

- Be extremely selective. You only need a few plants. A Taoist garden is not a riot of flowerbeds. It includes a few dramatic flowers placed in a way that makes them most beautiful. For example, a single clematis climbing a trellis shows the beauty of the blossoms and the foliage.
- Use native plants and local methods of cultivation to create a garden that can survive and thrive without the use of chemicals. Using native plants also helps you capture the spirit of the area where you live, so that you can connect with it.
- Because staying in tune with nature is the essence of a Taoist garden, don't use harsh chemicals — herbicides, fertilizers, and pesticides — in your garden.
- Maintain a compost bin for your Taoist garden to reuse the bounty of nature. For more on composting, see Chapter 7.

Take special care with what you plant near walkways. You don't want plants reaching out to touch your guests.

In Taoist gardens, perennial plants and long-lived trees and shrubs are preferred for their longevity; annuals are less popular, because they come and go each year.

Putting away the clippers

Although some Feng Shui gardeners clip their hedges and bushes into auspicious Feng Shui shapes, don't try this in your Taoist garden. The plants are allowed to grow naturally. Take this into consideration as you plan and plant; unpruned bushes and shrubs take up space differently from carefully clipped hedges.

For example, although you may be dying to plant wild forsythia, if your area is small or hemmed in by walks, a smaller bush or an arrangement of flowers is more appropriate. Save the forsythia for an area big enough to accommodate the long, draping branches.

Just because the natural is prized in a Taoist garden doesn't mean you don't have to maintain the garden, though. You still need to pick up clutter, clear undergrowth, and remove dying or dead plants, which can otherwise generate negative chi and create depressed energy. And you still need to prune dead or unhealthy branches from trees and shrubs. See Chapter 12 for more on clearing the clutter.

Unfortunately, appearing effortless isn't the same thing as actually being effortless, and a Taoist garden still requires most of the usual garden maintenance, such as mulching and raking.

Putting the pieces together

For inspiration as you plan your Taoist garden, go to a park or natural space that you love and note down what you appreciate most about it. Then apply that vision to your Taoist garden. Remember, a Taoist garden is just nature, slightly improved upon. So if the last time you took a walk in the forest, you stumbled upon a patch of wild strawberries on the other side of the creek, and you sat down and ate a handful, you can recreate that experience in your garden. But add a nice wooden bench next to the strawberries so you can enjoy them in comfort, and place a bridge over the stream so you don't have to wade across it (that's what we mean by improving upon nature).

A Taoist garden isn't a jigsaw puzzle, but you do have to put the pieces together. Start with a focal point, such as a tree you love, a decorative object you cherish, or a rockery that draws everyone's attention (see the section, "Creating a rockery" for more).

Creating a rockery

Very common in Taoist gardens, *rockeries* (or waterfalls; see Figure 17-3) combine stone and water to create a natural-appearing waterfall. Usually, the waterfall flows into a pond also rimmed with rocks — unless you happen to have a creek running through your property, in which case that's what the waterfall can flow into.

Photo courtesy of author

Figure 17-3: Native stones were used to create this garden waterfall.

A rockery gives more vibrant yang energy to the garden than a still pond does (and because still ponds are breeding grounds for mosquitoes, in these days of West Nile virus, they should probably be avoided), and it can be the focus of your Taoist garden. Read on to find out how to make your own rockery.

What you need

To create a rockery, you need either a natural stream running through your property (we realize this isn't all that likely, but who knows?), or a recirculating water pump and an outside water faucet/water source (much more likely). You also need the following:

- **Rocks:** You can find these at a local quarry, and at nurseries that specialize in pond landscaping.

  By selecting interesting rocks, you can create a visually stunning waterfall even on a limited budget.
- **Water plants:** Because Taoist gardens are supposed to look like they happened on their own, be sure to use plants that are native to your area and climate. The local nursery or water garden society can tell you which native plants will work best in your pond.

Designing your rockery

Design the waterfall and pond before you start digging up ground. (Yes, that should be self-evident, but . . .) Choose an area that slopes naturally so that the waterfall can pour into the pool without you having to dig too many trenches or truck in quantities of soil.

The waterfall should flow toward your home, not away from it, or else, according to Feng Shui, you symbolically drain the wealth away from your home — and by extension, your wallet. (Oops.)

However, if too much water flows too quickly toward your home, it can symbolize flooding and can seem symbolically threatening. (In some cases, it can be actually threatening if your area is prone to flash flooding.) Try for a gentle flow, even a trickle, rather than a great rushing river of water.

Keep these general rules in mind when creating your rockery:

- Use an odd number of stones. Multiples of nine are good luck in Feng Shui.
- Bury the stones in the soil; don't just place them on the soil. Avoid using cement or other fixatives, because they aren't natural. Burying the stones keeps them in place without using man-made chemicals.
- Alternate flat and upright stones for a natural look.
- Place the most weathered face of the stone outward. This type of character is prized in traditional Chinese gardening.

Seeing the garden from different angles

As you plan and create your Taoist garden, consider how it will appear from different perspectives. If you look from the kitchen window into the garden, you have one perspective. If you stand out in the garden looking toward the kitchen window, you have another perspective. Plan for these different views as you design your garden. You don't want the garden to look beautiful from the front gate and terrible from the kitchen window.

The Taoist garden uses windows, archways, and the like to frame the scene beyond and to invite the visitor through the garden. See the color section in this book for some great examples of how this framing works.

A Taoist garden is meant for people to use it — appreciating it from inside, not from afar. So buildings and structures are included to help guests get the most enjoyment from the garden. Decks and benches (sometimes seating is made from rocks) allow people to gather in the garden and enjoy their surroundings. See Figure 17-4 for an example.

© 2004 EDAW — photography by Dixi Carrillo

Figure 17-4: This garden is meant for guests to relax and enjoy.

Incorporating the house into the garden

The home and garden are seen as a single unit in traditional Chinese design. So instead of treating house and garden separately, you design them to be appreciated together. For instance, the windows and doors of the house open into the garden and bring the garden into the home. The walls of the house can serve as a setting or backdrop for plants and natural objects.

Considering the house and garden as one is also good Feng Shui. Focusing on making the house and garden one whole is a way you can focus on achieving balance and harmony throughout all aspects of your life. See Chapter 6 for more information on Feng Shui principles.

Placing the house in the center of the Bagua

Think of it this way: The house is the center of your life. So place the Bagua over your house and yard so the house is in the center sector of the Bagua, the T'ai Chi sector. Every other Life Sector radiates out from that center sector. The front yard, side yards, backyard, and house are all part of one complete environment.

As you design your Taoist garden, consider the Life Sectors in the Bagua and how best to enhance the chi in each area. See Chapters 3 and 6 for more on using the Bagua in the garden.

Designing a Taoist landscape in front and back

Because your front yard is probably part of a whole community of front yards, it needs to be a good citizen and resemble the other front yards. But that doesn't mean that you're stuck with planting Kentucky blue grass and leaving it alone.

A front yard can contain beautiful perennials and a few interesting rocks without being too different, aesthetically, from its neighbors. It can include a water fountain near the front door without getting too many raised eyebrows. Keep the front yard simple yet dramatic, and you capture the spirit of a Taoist garden without alarming the neighbors. Consider this the more yang, public garden, and treat it accordingly.

In the backyard, design and plan your more yin, private garden. Back here, you can be as exotic as you want, wallowing in moon gates (see Chapter 4) and entire collections of rocks shaped like turtles.

The front yard contains the Career sector, the Knowledge sector, and the Helpful People sector.

- Place a water feature in the Career sector because water enhances the chi here.
- Add the Earth element to the Knowledge sector; for instance, a few boulders, artistically arranged.
- Put a round ornament in the Helpful People sector, round being the shape associated with that sector. Or add some round stepping stones that lead to the backyard in this sector.

The side yards contain the Family sector and the Children sector. Parts of these sectors may also fall in the backyard. Instead of having a fence cut through the sectors, a more auspicious approach is to move the fence so that each of these sectors is either in the public space (side yards) or the private space (backyard).

- The Wood element in the Family sector raises the chi. Any plant symbolizes the Wood element, but a tree may be a good choice, as long as it doesn't block the entrance to the backyard.
- Plant a dramatic white flower, such as a lily, in the Children sector because white is the color associated with that sector.

The backyard contains the Wealth sector, the Fame sector, and the Relationships sector.

- Wood element is associated with the Wealth sector; plants symbolize the Wood element so any plant placed here raises the chi. Because purple is the color associated with the Wealth sector, a dramatic purple plant (wisteria, aster, violet) is even more favorable. However, because running water (as in a stream or waterfall) symbolizes wealth and abundance, and is auspicious in this sector, consider placing a water feature here, perhaps with a wooden bridge across it.
- A red plant (firebush, phlox) can add drama to the Fame sector while also raising the chi. Or consider putting a red or flame-shaped object or statue here.
- A selection of stones or boulders in the Relationships sector raises the chi; stones and boulders symbolize the Earth element, which is associated with this sector.

Chapter 18

Kitchen Garden

In This Chapter

- Finding the best spot for your garden
- Figuring out what you want to plant
- Creating a garden that lasts through several seasons

Nothing is quite as satisfying as slipping out the back door and picking a few ripe tomatoes to serve with the supper simmering on the stove.

Okay, okay, so none of us actually cook supper anymore, and even if we did, we wouldn't have it simmering on the stove in the middle of summer (simmering on the grill, maybe). But you know what we mean; nothing beats the taste of homegrown produce — and growing that produce is easier than you may think.

Many gardeners are starting to realize that the boring vegetable patch of yesteryear — now rechristened the kitchen garden — doesn't have to be the same old utilitarian setup it used to be. The kitchen garden has come out of hiding and is taking its rightful place next to the flowerbeds and butterfly gardens!

The kitchen garden is visually appealing and productive, making it a feast for the eyes *and* the stomach. When you design your kitchen garden according to the principles of Feng Shui, you bring even more blessings into your life. In fact, kitchen gardens are all about producing abundance in your life!

In this chapter, we get you started growing a kitchen garden that serves up all the beets and broccoli you can handle.

Placing the Garden in the Best Location

To make sure the kitchen garden you create is healthy and productive, take some time to consider the best place for it. Think about the principles of Feng Shui as you make your plans. Putting the vegetable garden in the Children sector is favorable, as is placing it in the Family sector. Also, keep in mind that the vegetable garden must harmonize with its surroundings. See Chapter 3 for more information on the principles of Feng Shui.

For your Feng Shui kitchen garden, practical considerations are as important as following the principles of Feng Shui. So just because purple is an auspicious color to plant in the Wealth sector and an eggplant is purple, if you hate eggplant, don't plant it.

Creating abundance with Feng Shui in the kitchen garden

The most auspicious shape for your kitchen garden is a rectangle or square, because the regular shape means that no part of the Bagua is missing — all the Life Sectors are intact and accounted for.

Most gardeners plant vegetable gardens with dimensions of 10 to 30 feet on each side, but you can produce a good crop in a smaller garden. In fact, the most common mistake beginners make is starting too grand and then not having enough time or energy (or canning jars) to keep up with their garden's produce! So starting small is definitely okay. Try a 5 foot by 5 foot plot your first year and go from there.

If you plan to lay your plants out in rows, keep the rows short so the chi doesn't move too quickly down them. Keeping the rows short also gives you room to walk around in your garden to tend and harvest your plants.

But where in the Bagua should you put your kitchen garden?

- It might do well in the Family sector of your yard, especially if you're hoping to make it a family project. (We're pretty sure you're going to have to do all the weeding, though.)
- The Relationship sector is a good choice, particularly if you garden with your partner. If you don't have a partner and would like to request the universe to send you one, cultivate

your kitchen garden carefully to be productive and weed-free, and you never know who might show up at your door asking to borrow a cup of runner beans.

- Another likely spot is the Wealth sector, where the abundance of the garden symbolically creates abundance in other areas of your life.

Wherever you place your garden, don't let unused veggies rot there. Rotting vegetables equal negative chi, and in the Wealth sector, for instance, they also symbolize money and abundance disappearing.

Making the garden user friendly

When deciding where to put your garden, consider how easily you'll be able access it when you're ready to pick some peppers for your plate. You may want to tuck the garden near the back door — but then consider the location of the compost pile. Many gardeners like to locate the compost pile near the kitchen garden so that they can throw plant material in it conveniently (and productive gardens produce a lot of plant material). Compost piles do, on occasion, have a bit of an odor.

So do you want to risk having a little smell wafting into the kitchen of an evening, or do you want to situate the compost pile away from the kitchen garden? Or would it be better to put the kitchen garden and the compost pile along the back wall? Only you know the answers to these questions. Take the following into consideration as well:

- **Sun and shade:** Consider sun and shade needs for your vegetables. You may have to plant in a less convenient location in order for your plants to remain healthy and produce food for your family. Most vegetables need at least 6 to 8 hours of sun per day.
- **Water sources:** Some gardeners like to clean their produce before they bring it into the house. This requires an outdoor water source (no, not the fish pond). Watering also requires water (we knew you knew that). Does it make sense to locate the garden near an outdoor faucet or well?
- **Herbs:** Finally, if you're planning an aromatherapy-herbal garden (see Chapter 13) in addition to your kitchen garden, you may want to plant them next to each other, or plant a kitchen garden that includes herbs.

Making these decisions before you turn the first trowelful of soil can save you frustration in the long run.

Planning for Your Needs

As you design your kitchen garden, remember that a visually appealing garden can be just as productive and nutritious as a utilitarian one.

- Ornamental vegetables add a splash of color and interest to your kitchen garden.
- Colorful vegetables are easy to find. You can purchase seed for yellow, orange, and red bell peppers; white pumpkins; purple asparagus; and blueberries and strawberries, just to name a few.
- You can mix vegetable plants with flowers to create an appealing kitchen garden that does more than produce cucumbers for the kitchen — it also produces bouquets for the table. See Figure 18-1 for an example of a garden that combines flowers and vegetables.

  Try planting edible flowers, such as marigolds, chrysanthemums, fuchsias, and violets. Not only do they add beauty to your garden, but they add goodies to your plate!
- Let some of your vegetables go beyond fruiting instead of cutting them back or digging them up. Broccoli and artichokes develop attractive blooms after they're finished producing, for example.
- The kitchen garden doesn't have to focus solely on vegetables. Fruits, such as strawberries, can easily be grown in a veggie patch. Some nuts, such as peanuts, can be grown in warmer climates.

Consulting seed catalogs

Before you can figure out what to plant, you need to know what's available. If you order seed catalogs (and then seeds and seedlings) in the fall or winter, you can design your kitchen garden and be ready for spring planting. Any gardening magazine has seed catalogs advertised in its pages. And take a look at *Gardening For Dummies,* by Mike MacCaskey and Bill Marken (Wiley Publishing, Inc.), for more information.

Photo courtesy of author

Figure 18-1: This garden includes flowers and vegetables together.

Your local extension agent or nursery ought to have information on which vegetables work best in your climate. Remember that native plants are more disease-, pest-, and drought-tolerant than exotic plants, so unless you really don't mind watching an entire crop fail, stick to the varieties that thrive in your area.

Consult the catalogs and draw up a list of must-haves for your kitchen garden, keeping the following points in mind:

- Keep each plant's special requirements (light, water) in mind as you choose.
- Beginning gardeners do better with hardier varieties.
- Those with less time to garden should choose low-maintenance plants.
- Gardeners in areas with arid, semi-arid, or drought-stricken climates should choose varieties that require less water.

Inventorying your eating habits

After spending some time deciding what to plant in your garden, do a reality check. While we're dying to someday plant the pastel-colored ornamental corn we once saw in a catalog, we know that it's not very practical.

Like most gardeners, we have limited resources of time, energy, and garden space, but even so, each year, co-author Jennifer is overcome with the need to plant everything from kale to collard greens, when in fact she hates kale and has never cooked a collard green in her life, despite living in close proximity to the South (she's not even sure she knows what a collard green is).

So consider what you eat regularly and would use most frequently from your garden, and plant those items. If you plan to can or freeze your produce, take that into consideration as well. Adding in a few ornamentals or oddities doesn't hurt, of course, but try to be practical.

Planting according to the Bagua

After you have an idea of the produce you want to grow in your kitchen garden and you've verified that it grows well in your climate (check with your handy local extension agent or nursery employee), plant the garden according to the principles of Feng Shui.

Just as your yard as a whole has nine Life Sectors, the kitchen garden itself has nine Life Sectors. So the garden goes into a favorable Life Sector in your yard, and then you apply the Bagua to the kitchen garden to determine where its nine Life Sectors fall.

Position your Bagua over your garden plot with the entrance to the garden facing the Career sector. Then use the Bagua template (see Chapter 6) to help you decide the most favorable places to plant your fruits and veggies. If your garden plot has no primary entrance, then position the Bagua according to true compass direction (for example, the Career or north sector actually faces north.)

Common sense takes precedence. If planting a certain plant in the Knowledge sector of the garden places it in partial shade and said plant needs full sun, plant it in the sunny side of the garden even if you think planting it in the Knowledge sector would be more favorable.

Use your imagination as you apply the Bagua to your garden:

- Maybe the Children sector can be the part of the garden your children are in charge of.
- Try planting your significant other's favorite squash in the Relationships sector. (Also, plant two of each type of plant here because pairs of items are better than singles when it comes to relationships.)

- If you plan to enter your pumpkins in the county fair, plant them in the Fame sector.
- Place arches in the center (T'ai Chi sector) of your garden and train runner beans or other vine-type plants to climb it. This creates a nice focal point for your garden and keeps the overall health and well being sector vibrant and productive (gosh, we bet you feel better already, don't you?).

Add pathways between each life sector of the Bagua for easier access to the various parts of your garden.

Don't forget to keep the Five Elements and yin and yang energy in balance, too. Include different colors and shapes of plants to help create this balance. See Chapter 3 for more information on balancing yin and yang energy, and see Chapter 6 for balancing the Five Elements in the garden.

Your kitchen garden can have objects in it besides plants, so use these objects to help bring the Five Elements into your garden. For example, you could place a small bench in your garden, or add a statue or two.

See Table 18-1 for more tips on raising the chi in different life sectors of the garden.

Table 18-1 The Kitchen Garden According to the Bagua

Plant/Object	*Life Sector*	*Reason*
Tomatoes, red peppers	Fame	Red color raises chi
Strawberries, raspberries	Fame	Red color raises chi
Bench (stone or concrete)	Relationships	Material associated with Earth Element; seating encourages intimacy
Pomegranate	Children	Symbolizes fertility
White kidney beans	Children	White color raises chi
Cauliflower, garlic	Children	White color raises chi
Tool shed (metal)	Helpful People	Metal element raises chi
Acorn squash	Career	Dark colors raise chi
Blueberry, blackberry	Career	Dark colors raise chi

(continued)

Table 18-1 *(continued)*

Plant/Object	*Life Sector*	*Reason*
Compost bin	Knowledge	Symbolizes improvement over time
Snow peas, bush beans	Family	Green color raises chi
Broccoli, watermelon, lettuce	Family	Green color raises chi
Pond or water feature	Wealth	Water symbolizes abundance
Eggplant	Wealth	Purple color raises chi

Keep a garden journal for your kitchen garden so that from year to year you can track what worked and what didn't work and make your best guesses why.

Giving some away

Giving some of your blessings away brings more to you. So don't forget to give your garden produce away to friends and family throughout the summer and fall.

Note: If you hear your friends running the other way each time you approach the front door with this week's supply of zucchini, you may want to rethink your generosity and find a different set of people to share with.

Some communities are delighted to accept donations of local produce for their soup kitchens and friendship meals. Local churches and community organizations are good places to ask about this.

Offer to share leftover seeds and seedlings with your neighbors. Most gardeners end up with too many and have to throw them out, but if a group of gardeners can get together before planting season to share the bounty, more can be done with less waste.

Keeping Your Garden Producing

If you're going to go to all the effort of planting edible plants, you want something crunchy popping up from the soil for you to enjoy come harvest time. So how can you make sure that your kitchen garden produces well for as long as possible?

Here's the dirt: Good kitchen garden production starts with good soil. Begin with a soil analysis before planting your first seed or seedling. Contact your county extension agent for a mail-in soil analysis kit, or purchase a do-it-yourself kit from a nursery or home improvement store. Local landscapers may also be able to provide a soil analysis for you.

Creating a raised-bed kitchen garden

If you have poor soil (clayey, poor drainage) for produce, you can create a raised bed in which to plant your kitchen garden. The process isn't too complicated, and it requires only basic carpentry skills. (If you know which end of the screwdriver to use, you're fine.)

You can create several small beds throughout your yard instead of one huge bed. In general, several smaller beds are easier to care for and more accessible than one large bed. A raised bed should be no more than 4 feet wide; otherwise, it's too difficult to tend.

You need:

- Four 1-x-12-inch boards. Use these to make the perimeter of your bed, so you pick the appropriate length.
- Wood screws or nails
- A shovel
- Some topsoil (amount based on the size of the bed; ask at your local nursery)
- Soil amendments recommended by the local extension agent or nursery

After you have the necessary materials, follow these simple steps:

1. **Select the site for your garden and lay the boards on the 1-inch side so that you create a 12-inch deep frame.**
2. **Screw or nail the sides of the boards together at the corners.**
3. **Dig and turn the dirt inside the frame. Dig about a foot deep. This ensures good drainage in your bed.**
4. **Fill in the frame with topsoil and any necessary soil amendments such as humus, sand, and manure.**
5. **Mix the soil and amendments together.**
6. **Plant!**

You can build a raised bed with other materials, too, including bricks, cinderblocks, and stone. These make good choices if you want to bring more Earth element into your garden.

You can then amend the soil or purchase good quality topsoil for your kitchen garden. See Chapter 7 for more on good soil.

Caring for the garden

How about some tasty pyrethin, butyric acid, and O, S-dimethyl acetylphosphramidothioate with your lettuce salad? Yeah, maybe not. You may be trying to poison the Japanese beetle in your garden, but you could end up poisoning yourself.

Feng Shui encourages the use of natural gardening methods; so give up those noxious chemical herbicides and pesticides. Turn to Chapter 7 for information on using natural gardening methods. Because native plants are more pest-resistant, pick those to plant in your garden.

Sowing the seeds

Vegetables are often grown in rows so that weeds can be easily hoed. However, you can also plant the seeds in groups. This works well in a smaller garden. After the plants are large enough, weeds can't grow as much (the plants are big enough to grab the water and the sun, choking out the weeds for a change).

Because not all seeds sprout, most gardeners plant more than they think they need. Then, as the seeds germinate, the smaller, less hardy ones are pinched off, or *thinned,* and the others have more room to grow.

You can plant fast-growing plants between slower-growing plants without threatening either plant. See the "Mixing it up" section later in this chapter.

Watering the garden

Water stress (not enough water) is very hard on vegetables. If you don't get about an inch of rain per week, you need to supplement with watering. Early morning is the best time to water a kitchen garden so that the water dries from the leaves (water remaining on leaves can cause rot and other diseases).

Drip irrigation is the most effective method of watering a vegetable garden. In this case, the water goes directly to the soil where it's needed. Soaker hoses (garden hoses with small holes drilled into them so the water leaks out slowly and evenly) are an example of drip irrigation and are readily found at garden supply and home improvement stores.

Harvesting what you've sown

Pick vegetables at the peak of their maturity. Take a look at the seed packet to find out how long before the plant is ready for picking. Mark your calendar! Then check every two or three days to get them while they're hot.

Root plants, such as onions, can be picked over a longer period of time.

Discard overripe vegetables (in the compost bin preferably), as they steal nutrients from growing vegetables.

Increasing the gardening season

You can increase the length of the gardening season by choosing early-producing crops, starting some seeds indoors in late winter or early spring, and by using cold frames throughout fall and winter.

Getting an early start

For early crops, start indoors 4 to 6 weeks before the last frost. Use pots or seed trays (called *flats*) for this purpose. These seeds need a heated area in which to grow. Further information on sowing indoors can be found on the seed packet or in consultation with the local nursery.

Growing in succession

Many crops can be grown in succession, depending on your climate. Your local extension agent can provide further information about which plants can be planted when. Also consult *Gardening For Dummies* for more information.

In general, early vegetables such as peas, bush beans, and some tomatoes can be followed by later vegetables such as peppers and squash. In late summer, plant vegetables such as beets, cabbage, garlic, kale, and onions for a fall crop. This way, your garden produces all spring, summer, and fall.

Mixing it up

You can also grow early and late producing vegetables together. For example, beet seeds can be planted in mid-spring with lettuce planted between the rows. By the time the beets have poked through the soil, you'll have used up all the lettuce. Spinach and carrots can also be planted this way (the spinach will be used up first.) Radish, which grows quickly, can be teamed up with lots of other plants, such as parsley and lettuce.

Using a cold frame

A *cold frame* (an enclosed outdoor bed) is used to extend the harvest season of hardy plants such as onions.

Cold frames can be used to help some plants survive the winter (overwinter) so they don't have to be dug up and can produce again in the spring. You can also use them to get an early start in spring. Cold frames are also great to help acclimate plants grown indoors to life in the wild outdoors.

The cold frame has four sides and a hinged, transparent cover. Plants are placed in the enclosure and protected from some of the wind and cold of the winter or early spring. The transparent cover allows the sun to reach the vegetables inside.

If it snows, the snow must be swept from the cover of the cold frame. Otherwise, the cold frame itself could be ruined, and because the sun can't reach the plants, they could die.

During warmer spring days, the cover should be propped open so that the internal temperature doesn't climb too high, which would endanger the plants' survival. (Remember what they say about leaving your dog locked in the car on hot days? Same idea.)

Purchase cold frames at nurseries and garden supply shops, or make your own. To make your own, you need:

- Four 1 inch by 12 inch by 4 foot pieces of lumber (you can also cut a 4 x 4 piece of plywood into four equal parts).
- Two 1 inch by 3 inch by 8 foot pieces of lumber, sawed in half for a total of four 1 x 3 x 4s.
- Some 2½-inch wood screws
- Two 2½-inch hinges
- 1 roll 6 millimeter transparent plastic
- Staple gun and staples
- Utility knife
- Drill
- Screwdriver

When you have what you need, follow these steps:

1. **Create the frame by setting the 1 x 12 boards on edge, so that the frame is 12 inches deep.**
2. **Secure the sides together using wood screws.**
3. **In the same way, create a lid frame with the 1 x 3s.**
4. **Unroll the plastic and place the lid frame in the middle of it.**
5. **Cut the plastic around the frame, allowing a 2- or 3-inch overlap on all sides.**
6. **Secure the plastic to the lid using the staple gun.**
7. **Attach the lid to the frame with the hinges.**

Using science and technology the Feng Shui way

Remember that the Feng Shui way is the natural way. Keep your eyes open to ways of working in your garden that are natural — for example, picking the bugs off your plants rather than squirting them with pesticide. When you must use science and technology, try to give it a Feng Shui twist.

For example, tomatoes need stakes to grow on. Rather than buying unattractive metal cages for your tomatoes, though, choose bamboo poles. Bamboo poles are more attractive, they represent the Wood element, and they symbolize good fortune.

When you must use a pesticide, think organic. If you want to keep the birds out of the blueberries, use natural cotton netting rather than plastic mesh.

Renewing and resting the soil

Your soil can't keep producing if all the nutrients are exhausted. You can renew the soil by testing it each year and adding what nutrients are needed.

Using homegrown compost can help your soil maintain high quality and good production. Chapter 7 has more information about composting.

From time to time, no matter how much you renew it, you need to allow the soil to rest. You can do this by rotating what you plant in your garden when.

- Many gardeners divide their kitchen garden into four equal parts. Three parts are cultivated and one part is left fallow, usually with a simple ground cover to keep the soil from eroding away. Each year, a different part is left fallow so that over the course four years each section of the garden has had a rest.
- Or, all four parts are cultivated, but each year different vegetables are grown in different plots.
- Finally, if you're growing some plants that require a permanent home, such as asparagus and rhubarb, you allow them to grow in one permanent plot and rotate the vegetables in the other three plots.
- You can also move your kitchen garden from time to time, although this can be a time-consuming and frustrating endeavor. However, if your crops start failing, it may be your best solution.

Chapter 19

Confined Spaces: Roofs, Patios, and Courtyards

In This Chapter

- Envisioning a garden in a small space
- Creating a tiny garden
- Nurturing your garden
- Fixing Feng Shui problems

If you're renting a small apartment or have a tiny backyard, is your only garden choice setting out a pot of geraniums on the front step? Of course not! If you have a rooftop, patio, courtyard, or even a windowsill, we've got you covered.

Small garden spaces have their own challenges, but also their own rewards. They require less maintenance than a full-sized yard, they're usually significantly cheaper and less time-consuming to create, and they can add years of pleasure and relaxation to your life.

Creating a small garden with sensational Feng Shui is no small feat, however. It requires care and advance planning and a little bit (okay, a lot) of self-restraint.

In this chapter, we give you hints on creating true Feng Shui gardens in limited spaces, and we give you tips for curing Feng Shui problems when you don't have a lot of elbow room to work on them.

Planning a Small-Space Garden

Don't be fooled into thinking that a small garden requires little thought or planning. To make the most of your small space, you need to devote time and attention to deciding what you want your small garden to do and how you want it to look, and then you need to spend some time plotting how to get there. This section tells you how to do just that.

First, consider the function of your garden. Yeah, we know you're not going to be playing football on the roof, so the types of functions your garden can have are limited. But you may want to create a contemplative spot, or you may want to create a productive vegetable garden. See "Choosing a theme and/or function" later in this chapter.

Next, determine how much space you really have. Can you create terraced flowerbeds to make more room? Don't forget that you need access to all plants, so plan for paths between beds and containers.

Finally, determine which plants will suit your needs. See "Choosing plants that don't mind cramped quarters" later in this chapter.

When planning, you also need to think about a space for equipment and supplies. Keep these items tucked neatly behind closed doors for the most auspicious Feng Shui — clutter and unappealing views are enemies of Feng Shui. An outdoor cabinet or deck box serves the purpose well — or place them behind a screen or trellis covered with a climbing plant.

The secret to successful small gardens? Be creative. Be very, very creative. For instance:

- If you have a small walled courtyard or balcony, use the walls for climbing plants.
- A railing on a small porch may be the perfect spot for clematis or ivy.
- Instead of the ceiling, try hanging baskets on the wall, Mediterranean-style.

See Figure 19-1 for an example of creative use of small spaces, and keep creativity in mind when planning your small-space garden.

Photo courtesy of author

Figure 19-1: This back step uses pots and hanging baskets to create a lush garden feel.

Assessing your situation

After you decide what you want your garden to do and how you want it to look, assess any special problems or conditions your small space may have. For example

- A rooftop garden is exposed to high winds. What can you do to help prevent those winds from wreaking havoc on your pansies? Maybe you could add trellis "walls" to blunt the impact.
- If you have a basement apartment, plants can offer a lift to the spirits but require special care and lighting to survive and thrive.
- Pots and planters full of dirt and flowers are heavy. If you're planning on placing them on a balcony or rooftop, make sure the structure is up to bearing the weight! Some balconies are meant for decorative effect only, making them unlikely candidates to hold the weight of six potted dwarf maples. Make sure you determine the load capacity of your rooftop or balcony

first; your builder or landlord can help. Your nursery can help you determine how much various plants weigh when potted.

- If you plan to hang baskets from a ceiling, remember that they're heavy, too! Your hardware store can help you with these calculations if your nursery can't. Be sure you have enough brackets to do the job.

Take your assessment of your space into consideration when deciding what type of garden you want (see the next section).

Choosing a theme and/or function

To create a successful plan, you need to decide what you want to do in your garden and what you want your garden to do for you. If you have a tiny space that you want to relax in, think about designing a contemplative garden. If you have a few kids who need to run around and let off steam, devote the garden space to that function. You can even entertain in a small space, provided that you don't try to entertain too many people at once (in fact, a small garden is just the place for quiet, intimate dinners with the cute neighbor who moved in down the street).

You can also plant a theme garden despite the small space. It's just a matter of choosing the appropriate theme. However, you probably aren't going to be able to combine more than one theme or function in a small garden, so choose wisely!

Zen garden

Zen gardens (see Chapter 16 for a detailed discussion) are especially suited for small spaces because

- You can easily transform a tiny patch of porch into a sand-and-stone garden, which is an important element of a Zen garden.
- All you really need is a wooden bench, a stone lantern, and a pretty plant in a pot in your courtyard and voilà! Instant Japanese-style garden.
- Because a Zen garden is simple and spare, choosing this style can even make your small space look larger.

Taoist garden

A Taoist garden (see Chapter 17) works nicely in a small walled area because you can showcase a few decorative objects: a small fountain, a miniature fruit tree, and a couple of nice stones in dramatic relief against the walls.

Aromatherapy-herbal garden

You can turn a small plot into an aromatherapy-herbal garden (see Chapter 13). An herb garden doesn't have to take up much room. You can even plant a small herb garden in a window box!

Butterfly and hummingbird gardens

You can definitely create a butterfly garden or hummingbird garden in a small space (see Chapters 14 and 15). Just plant the flowers they love, and watch out your window!

Kitchen garden

A kitchen garden (see Chapter 18) isn't out of the question, although you may find it easier to plant vegetables like tomatoes, which you can grow in pots on the porch, rather than squash, which requires a lot of room to run.

For more information about container gardening, including growing veggies, try `www.gardenguides.com/TipsandTechniques/container.htm`.

A nice compromise is to create an aromatherapy-herbal garden and supplement it with a few vegetables that can be grown in containers.

Applying the Bagua anywhere

Don't forget to adhere to the principles of Feng Shui even if your gardening efforts have to be confined to a few pots on your balcony. You can still bring abundance to all areas of your life by applying Feng Shui to your tiny garden.

The Bagua (see Chapter 6) can be applied to any space, no matter how small. So you can place the Bagua on your balcony, porch, courtyard, or tiny backyard. Remember to place the Career sector where the entrance to your garden is.

Use your imagination to raise the chi in the Life Sectors of the Bagua. In a large garden, you can plant a rhododendron in the Fame sector to raise the chi there. In a smaller space, that may not be practical. So think in terms of small objects as well as plants. A stone or shell in a Life Sector doesn't take up much room, but it does raise the chi.

Also, think of doubling up on your efforts. Crystals enhance the chi in any Life Sector. Rose quartz crystal gives you a double whammy in the Relationships sector because the pink color is associated with the Relationships sector.

And don't forget the miniature pond or fountain. Water features come in tiny sizes, and some are made for outdoor use. Or you can create your own water feature (think aquarium and pump).

All the principles still apply, such as balancing the Five Elements and keeping yin and yang energy in equilibrium — everything just functions on a smaller scale! See Chapter 3 for more on Feng Shui principles.

Carrying Out Your Plan

After you've decided what you want to do in your small garden, you need to put your plan into action. Think small and portable.

Selecting pots and planters

In cramped quarters, planting in pots and planters makes sense. They can be moved as needed and are portable — or at least more portable than a flowerbed. (An important consideration if you rent your home and move frequently or don't have permission to dig up the lawn.)

Remember, in a small garden, proportion is everything (see Figure 19-2):

- Massive pots overwhelm a small space.
- A large collection of tiny pots can seem cluttered.
- Pots sized and placed for maximum impact can make a small garden exciting.

Any container that holds soil and has drainage holes (or can have drainage holes drilled into the bottom) can be planted with flowers.

All plants eventually outgrow their pots and planters, so realize that you must replace or repot your plants every so often.

As always, good Feng Shui means using natural materials. Keep the following in mind when making your selections:

- Use pots and planters made of wood, stone, metal, and terra cotta.
- Place clay pots inside wicker or metal baskets to double up on elements — clay is Earth element, wicker is Wood element, and metal is Metal element.

- Pots can be painted, glazed, or left natural, depending on what you're using them for: A painted pot can raise the chi in your garden, but a natural one doesn't conflict with the colors of a blossoming plant.

  If you use colored pots, make sure the colors of the plants and the pots they're in work together according to the Five Elements. For instance

  - A good combination is made up of pink blossoms in a white pot set in the Relationships sector. White is associated with Metal element and pink with the Relationships sector. The Relationships sector is associated with Earth element, and Earth creates Metal, so all aspects are in harmony and support each other.
  - A red begonia plant in a blue pot in the Helpful People sector (Metal, gray) sector may send all the wrong signals — Fire (red) melts Metal, and Water (blue) extinguishes Fire.
  - Try a green pot instead — Wood (green) feeds Fire (red) — and put the pot in the Family (Wood, green) sector.

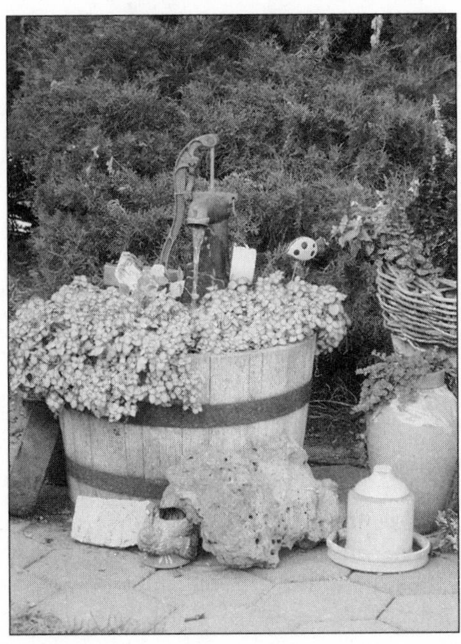

Photo courtesy of author

Figure 19-2: The variety of containers makes this small garden spot appealing.

How to plant in pots

Planting in pots is fairly simple. Just follow these easy steps:

1. **Place rocks or pebbles in the bottom of the pot to keep the soil from trickling out through the drainage holes.**
2. **Add potting soil.**

   The soil you use should be formulated for the type of plant you're potting. Some flowers, such as azaleas, like slightly more acidic soil than other plants. Your local garden store can help you figure out what you need.
3. **Plant flowers at the same depth they were in their original pots or trays.**

   Bulbs can be planted according to directions on the package.

   Keep in mind that you can plant more than one type of plant per pot or planter.
4. **Water.**
5. **If a lot of soil is visible, add mulch or decorative rock or shells for effect and to contain moisture.**

Making the most of a small ground plot

If you have a small plot of ground that you can dig in, you may want to combine both pots and flowerbeds. Using pots as well as flowerbeds gives you flexibility and may increase your gardening space. For example, if you have a small patio that looks onto a small patch of land, you can place potted plants on the patio and put flowerbeds in the land.

With a small ground plot, proportion is everything. A few small beds are more appealing than one large bed (and also easier to work in). Several small beds with space between also allows for better chi flow through the garden.

To maximize your space, think "up." Add a lattice wall for climbing plants (wisteria and ivy) or a small lattice arch. Place a water feature on the wall instead of on the ground to visually increase your space.

Choosing plants that don't mind cramped quarters

Just because your garden may be scaled down doesn't mean your dreams have to be! You can create a beautiful small garden with any of dozens of flowers, plants, and trees, as long as you think *miniature* versions.

Many dwarf and miniature species of your favorite plants exist. Some trees have a cousin that's a shrub, so you can get almost-but-not-quite-exactly what you want. See the sidebar, "Great plants for small spaces," for plants that may work well in your small garden.

When creating a container garden, you may want to spring for slightly more exotic plants than usual to give your garden more sizzle for the space. More temperamental plants can be brought indoors and cared for there when gloomy weather approaches then returned to the outdoor garden when skies are clear.

Great plants for small spaces

The following plants work well in containers or small plots:

- Begonia
- Chrysanthemum
- Forget-me-not
- Fuchsia
- Hydrangea
- Impatiens
- Juniper
- Lily-of-the-Valley
- Lobelia
- Lotus
- Marigold
- Nasturtium
- Pansy
- Petunia
- Rhododendron
- Snapdragon
- Verbena

These vegetable plants are great for small spaces:

- Dwarf fruit trees, such as lemon, orange, and apple
- Oregano
- Peppers
- Rosemary
- Sage
- Strawberries
- Thyme
- Tomatoes

Keep in mind that moving a plant in and out and in and out can be a bit hard on it; so keep the transfers to a minimum. Move it indoors in the winter and then outdoors in the spring, and you'll be fine.

Your neighborhood garden center should have plenty of information about which plants work best in your climate. They should also be able to tell you all you want to hear about small plants suited for a small garden.

Incorporating other objects

Your small garden can incorporate objects other than plants. Water features, birdbaths, statues, and other decorative elements can be incorporated to give full-scale impact to a small-scale space. For best effect, pick a few really terrific decorative objects and let them be the focus. See Figure 19-3 for more on dressing up small spaces.

These objects can be used to raise the chi in the various Life Sectors. For example, water features can be used in the Career sector because it is associated with the Water element. A stone statue can go in the Knowledge sector because stone is an Earth element, and Earth element is related to the Knowledge sector. See Chapter 6 for more information.

Figure 19-3: Decorative objects spice up small spaces.

Caring for a Small Garden

A smaller garden can save you hours of labor and still reward you with hours of pleasure. But remember that the small garden still needs to be kept tidy, and that plants need to be strong and healthy (dead and dying plants generate negative chi and should be destroyed).

Perennials may need to be replaced every few years. Their care is straightforward: Each year, replace the top few inches of soil with new topsoil and compost. Throughout the season, remove dead leaves and deadheads. When they're past their blooming prime, rotate them to a less obvious part of the garden.

Trees and shrubs need to be pruned annually (except topiary shrubs, which may require a little more attention). Remove deadheads from shrubs that flower. Every few years, they may need to be repotted.

See Figure 19-4 for a great use of small space.

Photo courtesy of author

Figure 19-4: Simply sensational small garden surprise!

Curing Feng Shui Problems in a Small Space

When room is tight, use creativity to perform Feng Shui fixes. So if the chi isn't moving smoothly and freely throughout your garden, use some of these fixes, called *cures,* to raise the chi and put things right. See Chapter 12 for more information on cures.

In a small garden, you're likely to have problems with chi getting stuck, because it can't move smoothly and freely about the space. So cures that have to do with creating more yang energy can help.

Remember how important intention is. Intention is stating your goals for any cure that you apply to your garden. So, for example, if you want to bring more abundance into your life, and you decide that planting a purple coneflower in your Wealth sector will raise the chi there, as you're planting the coneflower, you say to yourself (or the world), "By planting this purple coneflower in the Wealth sector in my garden, I am inviting abundance into my life." Let your intentions do much of your work for you. See Chapter 2 for more information on intentions.

Also, don't forget that you need to keep the Five Elements in balance even in a small garden. See Chapter 3 for more information on the Five Elements.

Again, be creative. If you need more Metal element for balance and don't want to paint everything white (the color associated with Metal element), try creating wire sculptures to bring a little metal into the garden without overwhelming it. Or bring in a small metal sundial. (Any metal object symbolizes the Metal element.)

See Table 19-1 for small garden problems and their cures. See Chapter 12 for more on curing Feng Shui problems.

Table 19-1 Curing Feng Shui Problems in a Small Garden

Problem	*Cure*
Chi doesn't move freely among pots.	Group pots together, but not so tightly that chi can't circulate. Or clear the clutter.
Chi moves too swiftly in the garden.	Round pots can calm chi.

Problem	Cure
Chi stagnates.	Square pots or planters can be used to raise the chi.
Chi moves too slowly.	Create a straight path with a series of pots in a row. The pots and plants should be similar for this to work.
Yin energy overwhelms the garden.	Place small glass ornaments in the garden to raise the chi. Or, add a water feature to enhance the chi. See Figure 19-5.
Negative chi is directed toward the garden.	Wind chimes can break up the negative chi. Or, a mirror can reflect the negative chi away from the garden while also making the garden appear larger.
One element dominates.	Use a color cure by installing brightly colored pots in colors associated with other elements.

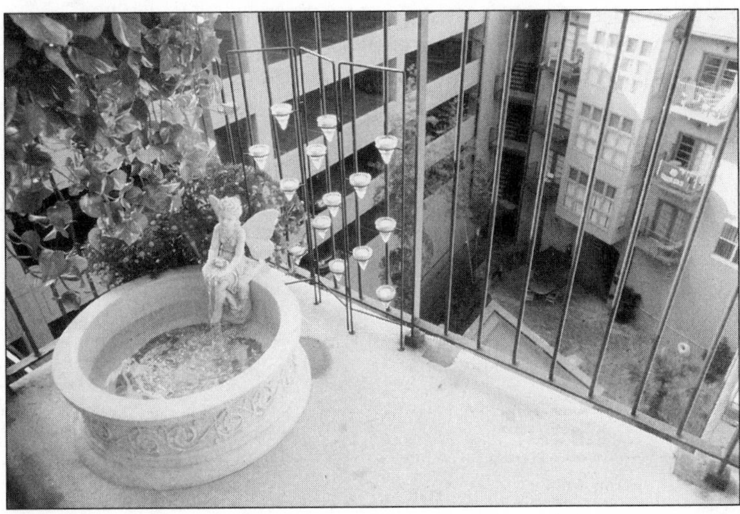

Figure 19-5: This water feature works fine on a balcony.

For renters: Getting permission to plant

People who rent houses, duplexes, and apartments with patches of ground attached often itch to garden but think their landlords will just say "No." Often, they're pleasantly surprised when they find out that the property owner is more than happy to let them plant a garden as long as they maintain it.

In fact, co-author Jennifer was once told by a landlord that he wanted to rent only to a gardener who was willing to keep the garden in his rental house shipshape!

If you're a renter, keep the following in mind:

- **Ask and ye shall receive.** Get permission before you do any digging. It helps to have some proof that you have a green thumb, such as a pot of geraniums flourishing on your windowsill.
- **Know what to expect.** The landlord may have definite ideas about what's okay to plant and what's not, or she may have specific ideas about what the garden should look like. Find this out before you spend all day planting a garden.
- **Remember you have to leave it behind.** If you're only planning to stay for a year or two, keep your garden simple. Otherwise, you may be sorry that all of those hours of hard work will benefit someone else after you're gone. (Or maybe that idea pleases you, and that's okay, too.)
- **If the landlord says, "No dice," be creative.** Use pots and planters instead of digging in the dirt. Find out whether the city will let you use the vacant lot down the street for your kitchen garden. Borrow a friend's yard.

Part V
The Part of Tens

The 5th Wave
By Rich Tennant
I told you not to stare at yourself in that thing while you're cutting the grass!

In this part . . .

Is your garden in dire straights? You need some quick fixes for bringing abundance (or at least tomatoes) back into your life? In this part, we give you the essential Feng Shui equipment you need to increase abundance in the garden, cure common chi flow problems, and create harmony.

Chapter 20

Ten Ways to Increase Abundance in Your Garden

In This Chapter

- Setting your intentions
- Raising the chi to raise the prosperity
- Letting chi in

We called this chapter "Ten Ways to Increase Abundance in Your Garden," but we could also have called it "Ten Ways to Increase Abundance in Your Life" or even "Ten Ways to Fatten Your Wallet." (We're thinking maybe that's what we should call this book so we can sell lots of copies and fatten our own wallets.)

The point, and we do have one, is that if you welcome abundance and prosperity into your garden, you're symbolically welcoming it into your life. And when we say *abundance,* we mean everything from having lots of good friends in the neighborhood to having lots of spending money in the bank. So when your garden's growing beautifully, your future's looking pretty good, too.

Some people are a little shy about asking for more. They think maybe they don't deserve it or that if they ask for it, they may never get it. Nothing could be further from the truth. Having abundance in your life means only good things for you and for those around you. And the only way you can get those good things is if you ask for them.

Knowing What You Want

The song goes, "You can't always get what you want," and that's true especially if you don't *know* what you want. So the key to creating abundance in your garden is: Know what you want. Then you can focus your attention and energy on getting it. If you don't know that you want daylilies and irises in your garden, you can't plant them, and that makes it a little hard for them to pop up in the spring.

The same goes for abundance in your life. If it really is more cash you're looking for, then know that and go for it. If you're just hoping this year's crop of zucchini doesn't fail, that works, too.

Saying What You Want

When you know you want abundance, speak your specific intention out loud. As you plant those zucchini seeds, say, "These seeds will soon grow into delicious zucchinis that I can share with my friends and neighbors. My abundant garden symbolizes abundance in all areas of my life."

Or something like that (we're not saying we're speechwriters). The point is, you have to name it to claim it.

Place a rock or other object with your request written on it in your garden. A simple word like *blessings* or *abundance* is all you need. You can create your own blessings boulder by simply painting the word onto a stone or rock and then varnishing it to keep it from fading.

Inviting Chi

You have to ask the abundance into your garden. The way to do that is to ensure that chi gets into your garden. If chi can get in and move about, abundance follows.

If your garden is all closed off, you're symbolically closing yourself off, too. If you want blessings and abundance in your life, then open up a bit.

Make sure nothing blocks the entrance to your garden. Remember, the entrance is the Mouth of Chi (see Chapter 4). It's how chi gets into your garden. It helps determine the type of chi that gets in. Don't fool around with the Mouth of Chi, or negative, cutting energy might be headed your way!

If your garden has a gate, make sure yours is open work or that you leave it ajar at least occasionally to let chi in. Yes, this may mean getting a friendly visit from the neighborhood stray dog, but everything has a price, even abundance.

Make especially sure that nothing blocks the Wealth sector (see the section "Playing with the Color Purple" later in this chapter).

Always start by clearing the clutter. This makes a huge impact immediately and opens things up physically and energetically for good blessing to come your way. Also, you're less likely to trip over something and hurt yourself. That's a blessing, right?

Playing With the Color Purple

Using the Bagua, find the Wealth sector of your garden. Raising the chi in this sector brings more abundance into your life and into your garden.

The entrance to your garden aligns with the Career sector of the Bagua. Chapter 6 discusses in detail how to apply the Bagua to your garden.

The color purple is associated with the Wealth sector. To raise the chi in the sector, you can plant flowers with purple blossoms — the blossoming flowers welcome abundance into your life.

State your intentions as you plant the flowers. "By planting these purple tulips, I enhance the chi in this sector and bring more abundance to my garden." Or something like that. See our disclaimer earlier in the chapter. (We're not speechwriters.)

Think begonias, purple sage, lavender, petunias, pansies, wisteria, and more (all in shades of purple).

Wooden You Know?

Because the Wood element is associated with the Wealth sector, making sure you have plenty of Wood element in the sector can help ensure abundance. Wood raises the chi. See Chapter 3 for more information on the Five Elements.

All plants represent the Wood element. So any plant increases the chi in this sector.

Here are a few tips for applying the Wood element to the Wealth sector:

- Choose woody plants for more emphasis.
- Wood furniture, such as bamboo and wicker, also increases the Wood element in this sector.
- The color green is associated with Wood element, so green foliage enhances the chi.
- Keep the Metal element to a minimum, as Metal destroys Wood.

Watering Your Wealth

Water is also a good way to raise the chi in your Wealth sector.

The Water element nurtures the Wood element — and the Wood element is associated with the Wealth sector — which is why adding water to your Wealth sector enhances the chi. Whew. Got that?

Choose running water flowing towards your home. This symbolizes abundance and wealth flowing toward you. Needless to say, a thundering river of water headed toward your house is *not* auspicious. Choose a gentle flowing water fountain or a trickle of a stream. A pond with a waterfall is always a good choice.

Goldfish also symbolize abundance, so be sure to place goldfish in the water feature. Nine is thought to be a lucky number. If one of the nine goldfish is black, so much the better — that black goldfish attracts bad luck away from you.

Dark colors, such as dark blue and black, are associated with the Water element, so adding these colors can enhance the effectiveness of the Water element in the Wealth sector.

Planting a Money Tree

Healthy plants in your Wealth sector create positive chi that boosts the blessings in your life (see the earlier section "Wooden You Know?").

One way to enhance the chi with a plant is to choose and plant a special money tree in this corner of the yard. The money tree symbolizes the abundance and blessings you'd like to have in your life.

You plant it specifically for the purpose of bringing abundance (specifically money) into your life.

Remember to state your intentions as you plant it.

Pick a tree that has leaves shaped like coins to symbolize growing money:

- In warmer climates, *crassula ovata,* also called jade plant or money tree, is a nice bet. A succulent (cactus-like plant), it has deep green foliage and blossoms in mid-winter with pink, purple, and white flowers.
- For less temperate climates, *lunaria annua,* also called honesty, moonwort, silver dollar, and money plant, is a good bet. It has purple blossoms, making it a very nice choice for the Wealth sector.

Lighting Your Wealth Lamp

Lighting raises the chi in your Wealth sector, so light that puppy up!

If you don't have pathway lighting or outdoor lighting here, think about adding some. Don't forget tiki torches and candles.

Anything that sheds light on the sector is good for your chi and for your blessings!

Thanking the Universe

When something good happens in your life, don't forget to thank the universe for it! If you did nice things for people who never acknowledged them, you'd stop doing nice things after a while. The universe is the same way.

You can create a regular ritual for thanking the universe for the abundance in your garden and in your life. Maybe each morning as you sip a cup of tea on your porch, you can look out into your garden and say, "Thank you."

Or you can remember to thank the universe at special times. For example, at harvest time, you can make a short prayer or toast or speech to whatever deity you choose (or just the universe itself). The universe appreciates the gesture and sends more blessings your way.

A long time ago, someone convinced co-author Jennifer to thank the universe every day, and gave her the words to a simple expression of gratitude: "Thank you for everything. I have no complaints whatsoever." Each day, without fail, Jennifer makes this statement. Of course, sometimes she's slightly sarcastic when she says it, but she says it anyway.

Passing It Along

Abundance is meant to be shared with others, not hoarded for yourself. So the best way to ensure blessing in your garden (and your life) is to pass the abundance along.

When you have extra pears and tomatoes, give them away. Or if someone comments to you how much she loves fresh red peppers, give her some from your garden (even if they're not extra). Passing blessings along makes the universe very happy.

Chapter 21

Ten Cures for Chi Flow Problems in the Garden

In This Chapter

- Clearing the clutter
- Inviting living energy in
- Seeking sound

The free and easy movement of *chi* (life energy) through the garden is essential to good Feng Shui. Without it, your garden doesn't produce as abundantly, and your own energy is negatively affected.

Unfortunately, even with your best intentions, sometimes chi movement isn't as good as it could be. Although you can prevent many chi problems with good planning, some of them come along unexpectedly and need to be fixed, or *cured.* Fortunately, most Feng Shui cures are pretty simple and straightforward. You don't have to take a lot of time, money, or energy to place them.

If you suspect you have chi flow problems, you're probably right. Your instincts are usually on target, so listen to them.

To spot potential chi flow problems, imagine chi as a river flowing and meandering through your garden:

- Certain places in your garden block the free and easy flow of chi, making them trouble spots. Examples of such places are clumps of trees and undergrowth or solid fences and gates.
- Other places can cause the chi to collect and stagnate (think of an algae-covered pond). Empty corners of the garden often cause this problem.

- Too much flat, empty space in your garden can cause the chi to move through too quickly, making it difficult for the chi to do its work of bringing positive energy and abundance into your life.

If you have any of these problems, we've got some quick cures for you.

Clearing the Clutter

The number one cure for chi movement problems is clearing the clutter. That means getting rid of debris, raking up leaves, composting grass clippings and other organic matter, cutting down undergrowth and overgrowth, and otherwise caring for and maintaining your garden. Make sure that you

- Pick up the trash that gets blown into your yard (pay a kid to do this if you must).
- If you have pets, dispose of their yard waste regularly. (If you can encourage them to use only one spot in the yard, so much the better.)
- Keep the grass mowed and the weeds pulled (pay a kid . . .).
- Do annual maintenance on your plants: deadhead blossoms (pinch off dead flowers), pull up annuals, and dig up bulbs, if necessary.
- Get rid of dead and dying plants. If they're diseased, discard them. Otherwise, compost them.

Keeping the garden clutter-free and well maintained helps the chi movement. It also helps you enjoy your garden more. Nothing gives you a headache faster than seeing dead leaves piled up under all the trees.

Placing a Bagua

The Feng Shui octagon, called the *Bagua,* is a powerful symbol. (See Chapter 3 for more information.) If you place a Bagua in the garden (and we mean put an actual, physical Bagua in the garden), it raises the chi and aids its movement.

You can use anything eight sided: an eight-sided bench circling a tree, an eight-sided herb wheel (maybe we should call it an herb octagon), an outdoor Bagua mirror placed on the gate to deflect negative chi from entering the garden. Any decorative object with eight sides works just fine.

You can place the Bagua anywhere else you want to. Place it where you've got chi problems, or place it where you think it looks pretty. Either way is fine.

Bagua mirrors that deflect negative chi from entering the garden are traditionally meant for outdoor use only. Don't bring them indoors to serve the same purpose. Instead, use a regular mirror indoors to raise the chi.

Using the Power of Intention

As you place cures in your garden to ensure the free flow of chi, remember to use them with *intention.* In other words, use the power of your mind to help out. An intention is a goal that you have; it's what you want (or intend) happen.

To cure a chi problem with intention, follow these steps:

1. **Determine a specific problem.**

   Don't just place a cure in the garden hoping it will work. You need to know what you want to accomplish (raise the chi, slow the chi down, invite the chi in, deflect negative chi away from your garden.)

2. **Choose a cure suitable for the problem.**

   For example, adding a water feature to an area with stagnant chi raises the energy level. (See Chapter 12 for more on Feng Shui cures.)

3. **Understand why you're using the cure.**

   Water symbolizes abundance and creates good energy.

4. **State your intention as you place the cure.**

   Say something like, "By placing this cure, I intend to raise the chi in my garden to bring abundance into my garden and my life." But we know you can come up with something better that's specific to your circumstances.

Coloring Your Garden

A powerful way to enhance the chi and to bring balance to your garden is through the use of color. You can use color to enhance the *yin* (passive) or the *yang* (active) energy in your garden. See Chapter 2 for more information about yin and yang energy.

Yin energy slows chi down, so if fast-moving chi is your problem, you want to concentrate on this type of energy. Yang energy, on the other hand, speeds up the chi, so if impeded or stagnant chi is your problem, focus on yang energy.

Bright colors are more yang, while darker colors and earth tones are more yin. Pastels can be yin or yang depending on their brightness.

Because plants and flowers come in practically any color you can think of, you're not limited except by your imagination.

If you want to bring one of the Five Elements into your garden (or into any part of it), use the color associated with that element. See Chapter 3 for more information about the Five Elements. For example, the Metal element is associated with white and pastel colors; the Wood element is associated with green. Although all plants symbolize the Wood element, you can use their blossoms and coloring to symbolize other elements, too.

The Life Sectors of the Bagua also have colors associated with them. See Chapters 3 and 6 for more information about the Bagua and the Life Sectors. So if you want to raise the chi in a particular Life Sector, plant a flower or place a decorative object of that color in that sector. For example, dark blue in the Career sector enhances that sector; pink in the Relationships sector is good for your love life.

Inviting Living Energy into Your Garden

Nothing raises the chi in your environment quite like the energy created by living plants and animals. Attracting living energy into your garden is very Feng Shui. For example, making the garden an enjoyable place for your children to play in raises the chi. Letting your pets run around outside also raises the chi.

You can plant your garden especially to attract birds, insects, and other wildlife (see Chapter 11). Butterflies and hummingbirds are attracted to certain types of plants. By placing these plants in your garden, you invite good living energy into your garden. (Chapter 14 is all about creating a hummingbird garden, and Chapter 15 is about creating a butterfly garden.)

Water, Water, Everywhere

Water is a cure-all for chi problems. Adding a water feature, especially one with running water, raises the chi in your garden. A water feature doesn't have to be complicated or expensive. A simple fountain works wonders. A more sophisticated waterfall with a pond (see Chapter 17) also imports good energy into the garden, if you're up to the tasks of installing and maintaining it. (***Hint:*** A murky pond filled with dead leaves does not enhance your chi.)

Running water symbolizes wealth and abundance flowing towards you (make sure the water actually flows toward your home and not away from you). Running water also makes a pleasant, soothing sound that can enhance the chi in your environment.

Putting goldfish into your fountain or pond boosts the chi even more.

Using Your Nose

Fragrances and scents raise the chi in the environment and serve as a terrific pick-me-up. And the garden is the perfect place to find some of these fragrances and scents. An aromatherapy-herbal garden (see Chapter 13) may be just the thing to keep chi moving in your garden. Or, plant a few plants just for their fragrance. Place them where you're able to smell them — near your favorite bench or next to the kitchen door.

If you want to perk up the chi (and yourself), try:

- Citrus orange
- Basil
- Cardamom
- Jasmine

If you want to relax the chi (and yourself), try:

- Lavender
- Rosemary
- Marjoram
- Pine

Moving Around

Movement in the garden is good. Like living energy, movement or moving energy enhances the chi in your garden, and keeps it from getting still and stagnant.

Movement cures are inanimate objects that move (if they were animate objects, they've be called living energy). Examples include pinwheels, flags, banners, whirligigs, and running water. Some objects and shapes also *seem* to be moving and these can increase the feeling of movement in your garden. Think circular shapes, curves, and objects made from natural materials.

Sounding Off

Bringing sound into the garden raises the chi, as long as the sound isn't irritating and annoying. You don't have to install an expensive outdoor waterproof stereo system to get some sound going (although you can).

Try these other ideas:

- Running water makes a soothing sound.
- Wind chimes make beautiful music.
- Birds invited into your garden can sing lovely songs.

Adding Objects You Love

Objects you love also raise the chi in an environment — and make you feel good. Try not to add things to your garden just because you have them or someone gave them to you. Use them only if you truly love them and enjoy having them around you.

Imagine stepping into your garden and being surrounded only by the plants, flowers, and decorative objects that you chose yourself and that lift your heart. That's powerful energy!

If you need a cure for your garden, don't settle on the first thing that will work. Make sure you choose an object you love and can live with. For example, if you want to place wind chimes in your garden, don't just grab the first set you see at the discount store. Take your time to choose a set that makes a sound pleasing to *your* ear. Make sure the chimes are appealing to your eye as well.

Loving what you put in your garden is especially important if the object is large and difficult to replace, such as a tree or a pond. But go ahead and surrender to those things you do love. Co-author Jennifer once impulsively bought a tulip magnolia with fat purple blossoms for the front yard (although she fully intended to do something different for the garden), and she never regretted it. She no longer lives in the house, but still drives by when the magnolias are in bloom just to see it. Now, if only she had placed it in the Wealth sector!

Chapter 22

Ten Ways to Create Harmony in the Garden

In This Chapter

- Creating good relationships
- Using the Five Elements to your advantage
- Balancing the principles

Your garden should be a peaceful place, even if it's alive with activity. (You want to hear the kids laughing as they play, not screaming.) A harmonious garden reduces conflict and negative emotions. It can serve as a place for you to refresh and renew yourself.

Harmony in the garden is about nurturing good relationships with all the living things around you, including plants, animals — and people! Creating harmony in the garden brings abundance and blessings to you.

Here, we give you some tips for creating harmony and balance in your garden — to help bring it into your life as well.

Curing the Chi

The free movement of chi throughout your garden is essential to harmony. If the chi gets stuck or stagnates, it can create negative energy. If the chi moves too slowly, it can depress the energy in the garden. If it moves too quickly, it can jack up the anxiety level. Cutting chi can make you (and visitors to your garden) feel subtly threatened or attacked on an energetic level. Cutting chi is created when sharp angles or anything pointed "stabs" toward you. Obviously, none of these outcomes is good for creating harmony and balance in your garden.

Taking a few simple steps can help cure the chi:

- Reduce clutter.
- Maintain your garden.
- Enhance the chi by adding cures such as water, sound, and color.

See Chapters 12 and 21 for more on fixing chi problems in your garden.

Having Harmonious Intentions

Your intentions are an essential element in the success of Feng Shui. After all, if you don't know what you want, then it's kinda hard to get it.

So you need to have good intentions as you create a harmonious garden. In other words, you have to decide that you want harmony in your garden and in your life, and you need to work toward achieving it, while at the same time placing cures and enhancing the chi in your garden.

Intention is just the start. Action is also required! If you want harmony in your garden and in your life, quit arguing so much.

Spacing Out with Yin and Yang

In addition to the chi moving easily and freely throughout your garden, you also want a nice balance between yin (passive) and yang (active) energy. Balancing yin and yang energy helps create harmony in the garden. See Chapter 2 for more information about yin and yang energy.

To ensure this, you want to include a nice mix of different kinds of plants in your garden and you want to include areas of open space throughout your garden.

Here are some tips for balancing yin and yang energy:

- Think of plants as yang and open space as yin. You need both to achieve balance.
- Plants should have enough space between them so that you can see and admire each one individually. They should also have room to grow.

- Clusters of plants in beds or groupings should be balanced with areas of open space.
- Open areas can include grassy areas, walkways, pathways, and patios.

Finding the "Harmony Sector"

Okay, the Bagua (see Chapter 3) doesn't actually have a harmony sector. But it does have several sectors associated with your relationships to other people, *and* it has the T'ai Chi sector (the center), which is associated with your overall health and well-being.

To create a harmonious garden, be sure that all Life Sectors in the Bagua are in harmony with one another — that you've paid attention to all of them and have neglected none.

If one of the sectors is "missing" because you have an oddly shaped garden, symbolically complete the sector by placing a cure, such as a light. For instance, if you have a garden shaped like a triangle with the base in front and the narrow apex in back, you apply the Bagua and can see that the Wealth sector and the Relationships sector don't exist on your triangle. They can't because there's no room for them. So you need to symbolically complete your incomplete Bagua by adding cures — any cure that raises the chi can work. Add the cure in the spot closest to the missing sector. You can also make some gardens square or rectangular (regular shapes) by dividing them. For instance, an L-shaped garden can be divided into two rectangles by planting a row of shrubs or some similar symbolic boundary. Then you apply the Bagua to each rectangle.

You also want to enhance the chi in the center sector (the T'ai Chi). Placing a special group of plants that you love here can bring harmony to the garden and to your life. An open courtyard or meditation area is also ideal in the T'ai Chi sector.

Yellow, representing the Earth element, is the color associated with the T'ai Chi sector. See Chapter 6 for more information about the Life Sectors.

Harmonizing the People Sectors

To bring harmony into your garden and your life, you may want to bring some special attention to the people sectors. Because harmony is about relationships — you can't have conflict without having relationships and you can't have harmony without relationships — paying attention to the Life Sectors that deal with relationships helps you find the balance you're seeking.

- The Relationships sector is about your intimate relationships — your spouse or significant other. Making sure it's looking good helps you in your own life.
- The Children sector is about your relationships with your children and about their growth and development. This sector is also related to creativity. Keeping this sector a happy place improves the chances of a happy relationship with your kids.
- The Helpful People sector is related to travel. But the helpful people it's associated with can be anyone who can bring goodness and help into your life — the pet sitter, the doctor, your assistant at work. This sector sometimes gets overlooked because of the more attention-getting sectors like the Wealth sector.
- The Family sector has to do with your parents, siblings, and elders. Giving this sector the attention it needs helps ease any conflict you have between it and other areas of your life (such as your intimate relationships and children).

Don't forget that other sectors have people connected with them, too. The Fame sector, for example, has to do with what people think about you — your reputation. Your Career sector is about your success in the workplace — which isn't possible without the cooperation of your boss, co-workers, and clients or customers.

Balancing the Elements

Use the Five Elements — and create a balance between them — to invite harmony into your garden. For example, the Metal element enhances the Helpful People and Children/Creativity sectors. Wood element perks up the Family and Wealth sectors.

Metal can be symbolized with metal outdoor furniture, metal ornaments and decorative objects, brass plant containers, and related items. Fire can be symbolized with red objects, flame or triangle shaped objects, and objects that have to do with lighting, such as lamps and torches. Earth can be symbolized by stone, ceramic and tile objects, the color yellow, and square objects. Water can be symbolized with water features, the color blue, and irregularly shaped objects, plus mirrors and crystals. Wood can be symbolized with any plant or with wooden objects. It can also be symbolized by rectangular objects.

Add these elements to their appropriate sectors in the garden to help improve the harmony in your garden and in your life.

Shaping Up the Elements

Each of the Five Elements has a particular shape associated with it. Using those shapes in the garden helps enhance and balance the elements and brings harmony to your garden.

- Pyramids, flames, and triangles are associated with Fire element.
- Square shapes are associated with Earth element.
- Circular shapes are associated with Metal element.
- Irregular flowing shapes are associated with Water element.
- Rectangular shapes are associated with Wood element.

Each element is associated with one or more of the Life Sectors on the Bagua. Placing the shape in the related Life Sector does double-duty for you. For example, Wood element is related to the Family sector. Placing a rectangular object made of wood (a bench perhaps) raises the chi in more than one symbolic way.

Color Me Harmonious

Adding color to the Life Sectors associated with relationships helps raise the chi in those areas and brings more harmony into your life.

- **Relationships sector:** Add pink and you'll be in the pink.
- **Children sector:** Add white to raise the chi in this sector.
- **Helpful People sector:** Gray or silver enhances this sector.
- **Family sector:** Green helps keep family matters harmonious.

See Chapter 6 for more information on using color to enhance the Life Sectors of the Bagua.

Nourishing the Elements

Tap into the nourishing cycle of the elements to create even more harmonious enhancements when you have the Elements doing double-duty. For example, because Wood feeds Fire, a red (Fire) plant (Wood) in the Fame sector (associated with the Fire element) does more for you than a different set of elements in the same sector.

Some more suggestions:

- Because Fire makes Earth, a red (Fire) plant placed in a stone-framed (Earth) bed in the Relationships (Earth) sector can smooth out any bumps in the path to marital bliss.
- Earth creates Metal, so yellow (Earth) flowers in a brass (Metal) container can create good feelings in the Children (Metal) sector.
- Metal holds Water, so a white (Metal) fountain (Water) placed in the Helpful People (Metal) sector can keep people happy with you.
- Water nurtures Wood, so a water feature (Water element) placed in the Family sector (associated with Wood) can make this area even more pleasant for family members to gather in.

See Chapter 3 for more information on the cycles of the elements.

Picturing Your Loved Ones

When Feng Shui is used in interior design, people are encouraged to include pictures of their loved ones in the appropriate sector to raise the chi and improve harmony. For an example, a picture of you and your spouse on your wedding day would go in the Relationships sector.

But this approach isn't too practical for the garden (we have yet to see photo paper that can withstand Kansas weather). Instead, choose items that symbolize those relationships.

For instance:

- In the Relationships sector, you can place two cozy chairs to symbolize you and your partner being together.
- In the Family sector, plant a flower belonging to your mother or old Aunt Martha. This acknowledges the connection and strengthens your relationship with various members of the family.
- For the Children sector, create a decorative object with the kids and place it in the yard.

You get the picture.

Index

• D •

• E •

• F •

• M •

• N •

• O •

• P •

• R •

• S •

• T •

• Y •

• Z •

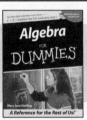

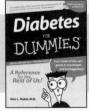

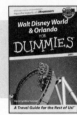

FOR DUMMIES®

HOME & BUSINESS COMPUTER BASICS

0-7645-0838-5

0-7645-1663-9

0-7645-1548-9

Also available:

Excel 2002 All-in-One Desk Reference For Dummies (0-7645-1794-5)

Office XP 9-in-1 Desk Reference For Dummies (0-7645-0819-9)

PCs All-in-One Desk Reference For Dummies (0-7645-0791-5)

Troubleshooting Your PC For Dummies (0-7645-1669-8)

Upgrading & Fixing PCs For Dummies (0-7645-1665-5)

Windows XP For Dummies (0-7645-0893-8)

Windows XP For Dummies Quick Reference (0-7645-0897-0)

Word 2002 For Dummies (0-7645-0839-3)

INTERNET & DIGITAL MEDIA

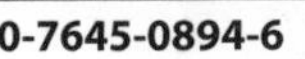

0-7645-1642-6

0-7645-1664-7

Also available:

CD and DVD Recording For Dummies (0-7645-1627-2)

Digital Photography All-in-One Desk Reference For Dummies (0-7645-1800-3)

eBay For Dummies (0-7645-1642-6)

Genealogy Online For Dummies (0-7645-0807-5)

Internet All-in-One Desk Reference For Dummies (0-7645-1659-0)

Internet For Dummies Quick Reference (0-7645-1645-0)

Internet Privacy For Dummies (0-7645-0846-6)

Paint Shop Pro For Dummies (0-7645-2440-2)

Photo Retouching & Restoration For Dummies (0-7645-1662-0)

Photoshop Elements For Dummies (0-7645-1675-2)

Scanners For Dummies (0-7645-0783-4)

- **Find listings of even more Dummies titles**
- **Browse online articles, excerpts, and how-to's**
- **Sign up for daily or weekly e-mail tips**
- **Check out Dummies fitness videos and other products**
- **Order from our online bookstore**

Available wherever books are sold. Go to www.dummies.com or call 1-877-762-2974 to order direct